A GUIDE TO COMPUTER MUSIC

AN INTRODUCTORY RESOURCE

By
Peter Donaldson

FOR APPLE II, GS, MACINTOSH & MIDI PRODUCTS

A GUIDE TO COMPUTER MUSIC© is
Exclusively Distributed By:

Sound Management
P.O. Box 3053
Peabody, MA 01961-3053

Printed in the United States of America by the
MINUTEMAN PRESS, Beverly, Massachusetts

CONTENTS

HOW TO USE THIS GUIDE

This guide is an introductory resource to help you identify and understand the components used for controlling sound and music with a computer-based music workstation. Specific product references have been focused on the Apple II, GS, and Macintosh computers with emphasis on organizing the Apple IIGS music system and computer-based MIDI systems.

Chapter One lists the goals of the guide, discusses the major developments in the field of musical electronics, provides basic information about music software, as well as suggests common applications of the technology.

Chapter Two provides information for the beginner: helpful guidelines and buying tips, planning forms for organizing a computer-based MIDI system, and illustrations about MIDI connections.

Chapter Three discusses and explains what parts are needed to organize the Apple IIGS as a computer-music system with digitizing hardware. Special emphasis has been given to the set up of the GS and popular music software suggestions.

Chapter Four identifies the components of a computer-based MIDI system with illustrations of several popular MIDI configurations. Basic information about MIDI channels, tracks, and sequencers has been included with a summary chart of leading product recommendations.

Chapter Five is a collection of product information for the Apple II, GS, and Macintosh products as well as the leading MIDI interface hardware and products that make it work.

Chapter Six is a comprehensive listing of purchasing contacts and leading resources in the field: MIDI dealers, how to books, purchasing catalogs, videos, magazines, MIDI associations, modem bulletin board services with MIDI forums.

List of Computer and Electronic Music Terms is an important listing of related terms used in the field.

CHAPTER ONE
THE BASICS

Goals And Objectives
Musical Electronics--A Technology of Creativity & Productivity
Understanding Music Software
Applications For Musical Electronics

GOALS AND OBJECTIVES

The fascinating fields of music and electronics have been combined to form the basis for a new phenomenon--*musical electronics*. As a tool, computer hardware, software, and MIDI instrument/devices can greatly assist and enrich our musical and creative abilities. The primary goal of this guide is to introduce the basics of musical electronics so that you may benefit from this new technology and to:

•Explain how electronic music systems can be used for a variety of applications--the Apple IIGS musical computer and computer-based MIDI systems.

•Enhance and encourage the creative process and the understanding of basic music concepts through musical electronics.

•Provide information and insight into the wide variety of music software and related produts for innovative use.

•Provide user set-up information for the Apple IIGS computer music system for composition, editing, playback, and printing of sheet music for the elementary and secondary levels.

•Provide basic guidelines for the development of a computer-based MIDI system for composition, editing, playback, and printing of sheet music.

•Provide reading and purchasing resources for continued development and budget/cost considerations.

•Explain and provide an up-to-date list of common computer and electronic music terms for user support.

MUSICAL ELECTRONICS

A Technology of Creativity and Productivity

Since the advent of MIDI in 1983, musical instrument manufacturers have inundated the market with a multi-billion dollar generation of compatible electronic devices. Through the evolution of synthesis, new tools have been discovered to enhance our creativity and productivity levels. Professional musicians were first to explore the use of electronics in music and, today, music educators, computer hobbyists, and even consumers are intrigued by these moderately priced musical marvels. Most name brand personal computers can be linked to the world of MIDI, and even stand-alone musical computer systems, equipped with sound chips, can generate crisp clear tone colors. You have heard electronic sounds for nearly three decades: in popular theme songs, pop music, advertising, motion picture soundtracks, and even jazz, classical, and new age styles of music!

A Little Electronic Background

The use of electronics for musical expression can be coupled to the movement of pop and rock styles of music during the 60's and 70's. As musicians searched for originality in performance and recording sounds, it was realized that through "synthesis," unique tones could be created/generated and modified to fit their musical persona. Electrical impulses could reproduce sound in a similar pattern as the mechanical vibrations required by actual instruments. The ability to synthesize sound set the stage for a new musical revolution. The use of electronic instruments and contemporary tone colors (abstract and immitative synthesis) artistically redefined the boundaries of creativity and productivity.

Through ingenous electronic engineering developers like Robert Moog, ARP, EMS, and other well-known manufacturers, synthesis evolved. Twenty five years of technological pioneering brought the musical electronics industry to today's level of sophistication. Like all new technologies, there were problems, and early synthesis was no exception. In order to generate a synthesized sound, a complex organization of patched cords (cables) had to be manually wired to each device—in and out of multiple modulator synthesizers, envelope generators, and filters, each extremely tempermental and valued at thousands of dollars. When a different sound was needed, it was necessary to repatch and tune the entire configuration. In time, as the field advanced, microelectronic technology yielded programmable synthesizers which allowed musicians push button control over the storage of specific sounds. Integrated circuits, custom music chips, and microprocessors, replaced the cumbersome individual modules eliminating much of the time consuming patching.

But problems with compatibility and synchronization remained and escalated with the introduction of new generations of musical electronics. Technical musicians would experience a multitude of problems when connecting differently manufactured devices. The connection of electronic instruments was desirable in an effort to create unique polyphonic and monophonic sounds. Consequently, musicians had to simultaneously play and manually control multiple keyboards and effect devices. Slowly, a series of electronic quick "cures" emerged such as synch-to-tape equipment which greatly helped musicians overcome technical recording and dubbing difficulties.

Throughout the 1970's, electronic instrument manufacturers such as Roland, Korg, Oberheim, and E-mu Systems developed and supplied the music industry with a generation of feature-rich keyboards and sound effects gear. Within ten years, the field of musical electronics revolutionized the music and recording industries. Musicians could expect changes in product lines monthly, each boasting of deluxe models, more conveniences, and richer sound patches. A full spectrum of creative tools enhanced their talents and yet they were still constrained by manufacturers' standards.

MIDI:
The Key To Musical Electronics

Musical Instrument Digital Interface, or MIDI was established as a cooperative effort, in 1983, by American and Japanese industries. MIDI became the communication standard to connect differently manufactured electronic devices. MIDI offers far more possibilities than was orginally realized. This international MIDI standard, a male/female five-pin DIN port/cable, is a serial protocol and by simply plugging in one MIDI-equipped device to another the compatibility problem was ended. The well-accepted MIDI communication link can send and receive a variety of musical and technical data. Through the MIDI port/cables/interface a variety of MIDI devices (synthesizers, samplers, drum machines, and other controllers) can transmit information about performance. The 16 channels within the MIDI interface transmits digital information such as: note on/off, exact keys and notes being played on a MIDI-equipped keyboard, when they are played and even at what degree of touch-release sensitivity, velocity sensing, and sound patch change within your MIDI device, as well as what control levers and pedals are used to regulate the pitch, timbre, vibrato, and volume. MIDI-equipped instruments can work in harmony just as if you were the conductor orchestrating all the members.

Since MIDI devices and personal computers both control data—they have become partners. A computer-controlled MIDI system can take on the exciting dimension of controlling multiple instruments and devices simultaneously, each playing it's own predesigned part or parts with single or multiple sounds. Powerful MIDI software has been developed to coordinate your MIDI device/s, computer, and interface. To connect your computer to a MIDI instrument, a MIDI interface is used. The MIDI interface is a computer-specific, user-installed hardware card that simply snaps into an expansion slot of your computer; and if this is not possible, a stand-alone MIDI interface device (box) can be connected to your computer's serial port by a cable.

The period from 1968 to 1988 represents twenty years of great achievements in musical electronics; the hardware developments would look something like this:
Minimoog—ARP 2600—TEAC 3340—E-mu Poly Keyboards—Roland MC-4—Music IC's, Oberheim—Prophet-5—Korg Polysix—SID Chip—Fairlight CMI—N.E.D. Synclavier—LinnDrum—Simmons Drums—MIDI—E-mu Emulator II—Ensoniq Mirage—Expressive Keyboards—Lexicon PCM70—Yamaha DX—FM and LA Synthesis (Electronic Musician, July, 1988). Future developments in this area

would appear to be almost unlimited. . .

Industry Leaders

Today, many new developer/manufacturers of musical electronics have joined the MIDI-related industry with their product lines and custom software support. Some of the leading organizations include: Activision/Mediagenic, Akai, Apple, Atari, Coda, Casio, Commodore, Dr. T, Electronic Arts, Electrovoice, E-mu Systems, Ensoniq, Fostex, Great Wave, IBM/clones, JBL, Kawai, Korg, Kurzweil, Lexicon, Mark of the Unicorn, MDIdeas, Microillusions, Music Quest, MusicShapes, Oberheim, Opcode, Passport, Roland, SoundCraft, StudioMaster, Sound Quest, Tascam, Technics, Sonus, SouthWorth, Voyetra, and, of course, Yamaha.

Musical Computers

In the last few years, stand-alone musical computer systems have become associated with the world of musical electronics. These computers are equipped with sound chips or add-on synthesis hardware and use music software to generate sound/music that is heard through the computer's internal or external speaker system. In other words, musical computers can generate sound without a MIDI device. A musical computer system, e.g., Apple IIGS, is primarily reserved for education, research, and the home, while MIDI equipment remains the professional and serious users' choice. The sound quality of computer music is "electronic sounding;" whereas, the sound emanating from high-end MIDI devices is more "real sounding."

Ending Notes

Electronic music, MIDI, musical electronics, and computer-controlled music are common terms for the electronic sounds or musical rhythms that are generated and controlled by a variety of devices. Musical electronic devices, such as MIDI synthesizers, samplers, drum machines, sound chips, and stand-alone musical computers, have rapidly become the economical method for orchestration of sounds in a simple to complex musical composition.

To synthesize sound, a specific sound's waveform is electronically designed and finely tuned. This waveform represents a sound's characteristics and will be electronically generated by the oscillators of a MIDI device or within the computer hardware. If an electronic sound is not synthesized, then an electronic sound can be referred to as a "sampled sound" in which a sound has been copied or transferred/stored into the memory of an electronic device or onto disk. These sound files, voice librarians, or preprogrammed sounds can be used over and over again and will sound exactly the same every time. Many musicians prefer to use a MIDI sampler instead of a MIDI synthesizer. Sound design is quite technical and requires sophisticated knowledge and engineering skills for programming synthesizers..

Since synthesized sound has been used successfully for more than two decades, more music educators, professional musicians, and amateurs have been attracted by the dazzling sounds. Within the last five years, the advancements in technology have progressed so fast that it has taken professional musicians and technicians countless hours to learn and use the powerful musical devices that are available. You, too, can start to learn and use these fascinating electronics by organizing a computer-based music system!

UNDERSTANDING MUSIC SOFTWARE

The leading developers of software are ingenious and devoted to their field. The continuous development of specialized music software has rapidly changed the rate of progress of the electronic music movement; thus, a wide selection of amateur, educational, and professional programs exist for all levels of musical interests. Software suggestions made in this guide generally apply to most major name brand personal computers, unless that specific program is exclusive to that computer or model.

Music programs are developed for a predetermined user group or level; namely, to assist you with composing and sequencing, in managing and being a librarian of specific instrument sounds/voices, to edit sound patches, to assist in music instruction (CAI), or to entertain. To further clarify these divisions of music software, these categories can help: Non-MIDI music software for home and education, music and utility software to support add-on sound cards, MIDI software for instruction, composing, sequencing, performing, and music software specifically designed for computers with independent sound capabilities. Educational music software ranges from basic sight reading tutoring programs and elementary composing programs to instrument finger training and the teaching of musical concepts through a MIDI instrument.

With a little time spent browsing through software catalogs and reading computer magazines, you will soon understand what music software should be used for a specific application. A good place to start, for example, would be the CODA Catalog which contains excellent product descriptions for its large collection of popular software applications. Passport Design Product Catalog is another source for professional composition and sequencing software for a variety of personal computers. Opcode Systems Musicware and Mark of the Unicorn software products offer professional quality software for Apple's Macintosh. Great Wave Software products are for the beginner to advanced user, and Electronic Arts' Deluxe Music Construction Set is an-all time winner. These few listings are just some of the exciting music software that exists; the only limit you have is the availability of a specific software package for your make and model of computer: Apple II's, GS, Mac, IBM, Commodore, etc.

The evaluation of computer software is a skill in itself. It would be ideal if all software could be used for a month or two and then purchased if desired, but this is usually not the case—the questions that remain are, "How good is the software for intended use? How fast can I learn it and achieve advanced user ability?" A good idea is to make a punch list of tasks you wish you could do faster and more efficiently and with greater control and flexibility. This list will guide you in the selection of the right software. To find the right one for your needs, it is quite common to experiment with several of the leading packages.

When selecting any kind of software always read the reviews, actually preview and use the software from a local dealer. The new, nation-wide chain of Egghead Discount Software stores encourage preview of software before purchase. If this is not possible, (mail order) find out the return policy for the software that does not meet your expectations. When you have found the right software, you will know! It may take you several software purchases. Some computer dealers have established rental software programs. For a small fee, which may be applied toward the potential purchase, you can preview leading packages. Ask your local dealer to purchase several popular MIDI software programs to add to the range of their rental program.

Computer software also offers fascinating options for the non-musician. A beginner may explore sound engineering with pre-recorded music on disk, or creativity music software has programmed artificial intelligence (AI) to assist in music composition without prior knowledge of standard musical notation—several software selections currently exist. (Instant Music, Jam, "M")

The following popular MIDI software suggestions will help you get started with home, school, and professional musical applications:

Passport Designs: (Apple II, Macintosh, etc.)

- Master Tracks
- Master Tracks Jr.
- Clicktracks
- NoteWriter
- MIDI 8Plus
- Polywriter/Utilities
- Music Tutor

Opcode Systems: (Macintosh)

- MIDI Editor/Librarians Software
- Sequencer V2.5
- Deluxe Music Construction Set V2.0
- CUE The Film Music Studio V 2.0
- Music Mouse
- Sonata
- Custom "Editor/Librarians" for Akai, Casio, Ensoniq, Kawai, Korg, Oberheim, Prophet, Roland, and Yamaha.

Great Wave: (Macintosh)

- ConcertWare+MIDI 4
- ConcertWare+4

Others Suggestions:

- Jam Session (Broderbund)
- Listen 2.0 (Resonate)
- Music Publisher (Graphic Notes)
- Practica Musica (Ars Nova)
- Professioanl Composer (Unicorn)
- Performer (Mark of the Unicorn)
- Studio Session (Bogas)
- Finale (Coda)

MIDI SOTWARE SUMMARY

- MIDI Composition Software
- MIDI Notation/Printing Software
- MIDI Sequencing Software
- MIDI Editor/Librarian Software
- MIDI Intelligent/Composition Software
- MIDI Software For SMPTE
- MIDI Educational Software
- See Chapter Five For Additional Info.

Call *Sound Mangement* for Passport and Opcode Systems MIDI Software.
508-531-6192

APPLICATIONS FOR MUSICAL ELECTRONICS

The applications of musical electronics are relative to the user's budget, equipment, and musical-technical knowledge. Essentially, MIDI equipment and musical computers become tools to compose, generate, record, or teach music and theory. Computer-based music systems enable you to accomplish greater musical tasks which would otherwise be too expensive or time consuming in comparison to traditional methods.

Basic Applications For A Computer-based MIDI System

- Compose and play music in real time and step time.
- Print sheet music and lyrics—dot matrix or laser print quality.
- Sequence, edit, and maneuver musical MIDI data.
- Record and playback saved accompaniments or customized data.
- Store and control a variety of sound patches/librarians.
- Sample and design sound files.
- Synchronize musical data to film and video soundtracks. (SMPTE)
- Control a variety of external devices (Mixing boards, controllers, lighting, modules, signal processors, etc).
- Live performance.

Basic Applications For A Stand-alone Musical Computer.

- Explore new musical ideas, concepts, and theories.
- Compose music using standard pull-down commands: (note value, copy, paste, cut, move, instrument selection, etc.)
- Create/select digital instrument sounds file for music composition.
- Print sheet music and lyrics.
- Digitize, edit, and playback any audio sound.
- Alter/edit digitize sounds for custom music files.
- Develop custom sound files for programming.
- Engineer new sounds through digitizing hardware and music software.
- Playback music and sound files.
- Introduction and development of sequencing and recording skills.

Educational Uses For MIDI and Musical Computers

- A personal computer and a synthesizer are learning tools in themselves.
- Create and explore with music theory software.

•Provides new instructional and illustrational classroom value.
•CAI (Computer Assisted Instruction) for drills, finger training, ear training, etc.
•Accompaniment and practice for a variety of classroom and home settings.
•Print sheet music for new or practice parts.
•Encourages user to compose original music.
•Supplies motivation for advanced training.
•Versatile equipment for a variety of ages and performing levels.
•Versatile MIDI and music software for all grades and user levels.
•Create custom sound libraries/waveforms for advance use.
•Make a recording.

The Musical Computer or a MIDI System?

There are advantages and disadvantages of both systems. However, MIDI-generated sound is far superior to computer-generated sound. MIDI equipment has been designed to be dedicated to the sole purpose of producing high quality digital sound. Specific musical computers, like the Apple IIGS, has been developed for multiple applications, and their sound ability is just one function. Primarily, the IIGS houses a special music chip for synthesizing called the "DOC" that will produce tone colors for a pre-determined user market. Some hardware and software "reviews" suggest that the IIGS is primarily a musical tool for education and home.

MIDI equipment and computer-controlled MIDI systems are the professionals' choice. As this technology continues to develop, the cost of electronic devices continues to drop and becomes affordable to the average consumer in which case more schools are implementing the new technology for introductory or advanced music training. Musical computers are an easy setup; a MIDI system will require more user effort. A computer-MIDI system will have hands-on use with MIDI keyboard and computer. The GS stand-alone musical computer will use only the mouse for musical data input, unless you add on MIDI equipment.

The applications of musical electronics are basically dependent on the proficiency of the user, the quality of equipment, and the degree of implementation. To achieve advanced-user ability, much information needs to be processed. There are numerous well-written manuals, guides, instructional tapes, and bulletin board service with MIDI forums available to help. Usually the development of electronic musicship is greatly assisted by the software manuals, MIDI equipment manuals, mini courses/lessons/consulting, and hands-on experience.

CHAPTER TWO
GETTING STARTED

Helpful Guidelines And Buying Tips
Computer And MIDI System Planning Forms
MIDI Connections

HELPFUL GUIDELINES & BUYING TIPS

This section, *Helpful Guidelines & Buying Tips,* has been developed to help you gain insight into some key points when getting started with musical electronics.

•Decide relatively <u>early</u>, in your developmental/ computer purchasing stage, whether you want to make music with a musical computer or MIDI equipment. MIDI is the professional choice but it is quickly finding its place, if not already, in the educational market. Musical computers are for school and home.

•Think ahead—develop a "plan of action" with specific short-range and longer-range goals for your budget, software and hardware purchases, self-development, and MIDI equipment needs. Develop a system that can be added on to when you are ready.

•When selecting a personal computer, these important options should be considered: open-architecture hardware designed for upgrades; internal operating speed of 4 to 20 Mhz; use of multi-task operating system/software; large variety of quality user-friendly music and productivity software; built-in MIDI port or MIDI interface hardware availability; regularly published user magazines for support and new product information; quality of the monitor resolution— color/ black and white; amount of internal RAM, amout of internal RAM needed for MIDI-user level, RAM upgrade costs; user interface—keyboard/mouse; quality and availability of leading MIDI software for composition,

sequencing, voice librarians, and, of course, the cost. Usually, you will trade off and purchase a system that will have more advantages than disadvantages. Manufacturers of personal computers used for music include: Apple's II, GS, and Macintosh Plus, SE, II; Atari's ST; IBM's PC, XT, AT; and Commodore's Amiga. (Rumor has it that some compatibles are not 100% compatible with MIDI interfaces and MIDI music software; always check with the manufacturer.)

•Purchase wisely. The electronic music industries are always coming up with something new, double check your references before you purchase; the "great deal" may not be so great after all. The dealer may want to reduce its inventory. Call the manufacturer directly and ask about new releases.

•Some personal computers are just better MIDI computers (Apple's Macintosh, IBM's PC's, Commodore's Amiga, and Atari's ST); likewise with a stand-alone musical computer, few are recommended. The Apple IIGS is one of the new musical computers that has software support.

•Keyboards, synthesizers, and other musical electronics are not always MIDI devices. Keyboards are found in many flavors and most merchandise and piano/keyboard/music stores sell a variety of these musical instruments. Non-MIDI keyboards are very intelligent in their own right, but are not a MIDI device. Non-MIDI keyboards have such features as: polyphonic or monophonic sound (play one note or several notes at one time), preprogrammed musical rhythms, auto-chord play with one note, sampling ability, multi-timbral, built-in drum kit/s, etc. These keyboards are usually intended for home use and non-MIDI use.

•A musical device must be labeled MIDI; to be sure, check the back panel of the device and look for ports labeled MIDI IN, MIDI OUT, and some have MIDI THRU.

•For the beginner, purchase low-end, easier-to-use MIDI synthesizers at first and then grow into more sophisticated and expensive units.

•Purchase and set up equipment that has a well-known reputation as indicated in this guide. Don't hesitate to order from companies that are not local; next day or two-day mail is standard shipping practice; use a credit card for convenience and for returning products if necessary.

•The well-known Yamaha line offers amazing MIDI keyboards and accessories packed with powerful features: preprogrammed sounds and beats, memory and track recording options, and even playback of prerecorded music recordings (3.5 disks). The advanced series of Yamaha DX, Roland, Korg, and Ensoniq synthesizers, to mention a few, are usually for experienced, professional use and offer quality sound.

•Common MIDI accessories include MIDI modules and controllers: MIDI drum machines and rhythm devices, MIDI recorders and sequencing hardware, MIDI signal processor, or phase distortion devices, MIDI guitar, bass and string controllers, MIDI mixers and network devices (MIDI Thru Boxes) and the most recent,

MIDI woodwind and guitar instruments.

•Music software is categorized as follows: Non-MIDI software used for home and education, software to support add-on sound cards, MIDI software for instruction, composing, sequencing, performing, and software for computers with built-in sound chips.

•Know what features you want in a sequencer: A stand-alone sequencer or sequence software. (See Sequencer Information)

•Do not become frustrated easily; learn to take small steps rather than large ones. Keep notes and files on the steps, procedures, and breakthroughs you discover—becoming an electronic musician is not easy!

•Structure/establish a specific part of each day for continuous development and practice; soon you may find yourself totally absorbed in your new discoveries.

•Many new MIDI users report this phenomenon when studying musical electronics: after a sufficient amount of time being confused, suddenly everything becomes clear.

•Find local user groups; music schools, and colleges are good sources. Consider receiving professional MIDI tutoring and consulting from experienced users.

•Subscribe, send away or write to the major manufacturers and software publishers and request new development updates/releases, newsletters, free informational literature as well as the recommended learning/reference guides and materials for your specific equipment.

•Use your modem for information, development, and for MIDI troubleshooting. In many major U.S. regions (e.g., Boston, New York , Midwest, California) MIDI bulletin board services are active and are extremely helpful. (See Chapter Six, for MIDI and telecommunications support contacts.)

•This guide does not include all the information you will need for technical MIDI recording. To help you gain more insight into music recording techniques, purchase several specific books and periodicals that are recommended in this guide. Most learning takes place with hands-on practice with your specific computer, software, MIDI equipment, and audio gear.

•You do not need to fully understand how to create and program sound patches within your synthesizer; most name brand synthesizers/samplers have hundreds of voice librarians available.

•Know the top ten MIDI products and how long they have been on the top; a change is inevitable.

•Always ask plenty of questions when selecting or learning about MIDI equipment and computers, and remember to learn the buzzwords in the field of musical electronics beforehand.

•No one MIDI system is a hundred percent perfect. No one MIDI system can do all for all users. But, a carefully planned-out computer-MIDI system with the right equipment combinations can come very close!

•Learn to be flexible; no technology is perfect and MIDI has its own limits. MIDI equipment and instruments specifications used today will change tomorrow along with the software.

•If you are purchasing from a local dealer, fully test, use, and understand the equipments' potential before you purchase. Know the overall quality of the sound and tone colors you desire. Judge the instrument's sound and user features (fullness/thinness and control features). Whether you are purchasing from a local dealer or not, find out the return policy for equipment that has not met your expectations. (Is there a 7-day, 30-day trial period?)

•Make a punch list of all music management functions you want your MIDI equipment and computer software to perform. This will guide you in the right direction.

•Continue to keep up to date with the industry—read and subscribe to several user periodicals to help you make wise selections for the proper hardware and software. *Electronic Musician* and *Keyboard Magazine* contain excellent feature articles about the business of making MIDI music. Watch for articles that signify change in user trends and new MIDI equipment releases.

•Plan your budget with this point in mind: You may spend more money than you originally planned!

•More often than not, the well-know MIDI dealers and software dealer can provide competitive pricing over the manufacturer.

•The estimated cost for a basic computer-MIDI system or an Apple IIGS + MIDI could range from a low, $3,000, to a high of $10,000+.

•Your requirements for hardware, software, MIDI equipment, and sound quality are relative to the total budget.

•Organize a spending ratio for the level of your intended use. A 30:30:40 ratio or 35:30:35 ratio could be used to start off. Allocate, from your total budget, a certain percent for a synthesizer or sampler, for audio equipment, and for computer harware/MIDI interface/software, as well as for countless accessories. Your computer and audio equipment "starting point" or "replacement point" are important budget items.

•MIDI keyboard and synthesizer trade-in and trade-up for credit is sometimes an option with music stores—this should be considered by schools and individuals experimenting with devices.

•MIDI product knowledge is one of the most important buying tips for the beginner. By knowing your product line-ups and what each one can do, you will gain the most out of your budget ratios.

•Once you have fully completed product clarification on a specific item, and you know what you want; listen for other manufacturer recommendations before making a purchase decision.

•If product support/training is not an issue, contack several equipment resources and check pricing and availability. Shipping MIDI gear is a standing practice by these distributors.

•New MIDI equipment is released monthly. MIDI devices manufactured by Roland, Korg, Kawai, Yamaha, and other recommended names can meet the needs of most users.

•All-in-one MIDI devices (synths, drum machines, and sequencers—Korg M1, Roland D-20, and the Ensoniq SQ-80 EPS) have many advantages. This integrated unit can be right for the user with a limited budget or for a musician looking for a system that serves as a workstation for creating/composing away from the studio. Schools would be interested in these devices as they are easy to set up for classroom use.

•If creating synthesized waveforms is not an important goal, MIDI sampler keyboards are packed with rich clear tone colors. The Ensoniq Performance Samplers are worthy of a test run.

•A beginning budget does not have to include every component of your MIDI system. A MIDI system can be built in stages. MIDI systems can always be expanded with a MIDI Thru Box, MIDI Switcher, and additonal MIDI devices/modules.

•Your budget should contain a spot for an audio signal processor. This money will be well spent when you add real effects to your MIDI music. Delay or reverb devices are a popular choice.

•Music software and sequencers are usually confusing at first; a higher level product will allow you to grow; a lower level product may need to be upgraded. It will take some time for you to learn the ins and outs of your sequencer, whether it is hardware or software.

COMPUTER AND MIDI SYSTEM
PLANNING FORM

The following planning forms will help you organize the equipment and projected cost of your computer music system..

COMPUTER SYSTEM:

Cost projection for entire computer system? $1000, $2000, $3000, $4000, $5000, $6000+
Notes:

Name of manufacturer and model of the computer system desired?   First choice _____

_____

Second Choice? _____   Used?_____

Amount of internal RAM memory needed_____? 256K,   512K,   1MB,   2MB, 4MB+.

Amount of external memory/storage desired? _____ RAM.

Number, kind, and size of floppy drives? (5.25/3.5)_____

Manufactuer and model of hard drive?_____

Size of hard drive needed?   20 MB, 40 MB, 60, MB, 80 MB+_____

_____

CD ROM?_____

Name and model of printer?_____

Quality of print desired? Dot matrix quality, Letter quality, Laser quality.

Laser printer: name and model?_____ Cost?$_____
Notes:

SOFTWARE:

Cost projection for start-up software? $300, $500, $700, $1000+
Notes:

Name of MIDI software for sequencing, Version)? _____Cost$ _____

Composition software (Version)? _____Cost$_____

Music printing software (Version)? _____Cost$ _____

Other music software (Version)? _____Cost$ _____

Other software for word processing, spreadsheet, data base, financial, learning, creativity?
 Cost $_____

Notes:

MIDI EQUIPMENT:

Cost projection for entire MIDI system? $1000, $2000, $3000, $4000, $5000, $6000+
Notes:

Name of manufacturer and model of MIDI Interface:_____
(Internal/External Tape/Drum Sync)
Notes:

MIDI switcher box?_____

MIDI THRU Box?_____

Brand name of MIDI synthesizer/s make and model?_____

Brand name of MIDI sampler/s make and model? _____

Brand name of MIDI drum machine/percussion? _____

Use of a hardware sequencer? _____Mfg. and Model_____

Name of MIDI module/s, controller/s?_____

MIDI cables?_____

Other MIDI equipment?_____

Notes:_____

_____

_____

AUDIO EQUIPMENT:

Cost projection for entire audio system? $300, $500, $800, $1000, $2000, $3000, $4000, $5000, $6000+
Notes:

Name of manufacuter and model of power amp? _____

Name of manufacturer and model of pre-amp? _____

Name of manufacturer and model of integrated amp? _____

Notes:

Name of manufacturer and model of multi-track recorder? _____

Name of manufacturer and model of speaker system? _____

Name of manufacturer and model of mixer? _____

Outboard devices—audio signal processors: Reverb effects? Delay effects? Equalizer? Other?

Miscellaneous supplies? Tapes? _____RCA cables? _____ Tools? _____Other? _____

Notes:

INTERVIEW FORM
Electronic Musician

Interview MIDI musicians, MIDI consultants, and MIDI dealers.

BACKGROUND DATA:

Name _____   Phone No: _____

How long have you been a musician? _____ What instrument do you play? _____

How long have you been using MIDI equipment? _____

Why did you become interested in MIDI? _____

How did you learn to use your MIDI equipment and system? _____

Approximately how much money have you invested in the entire system? $_____

Recommendations for learning a new MIDI system? _____

_____

Recommended Computer System Description:
(Manufacturer, Model, Memory, Printer, Software)

Recommended MIDI System Description:
(Manufacturer, Model, Synth, Samplers, MIDI interface, Drum machine, Mixer, MIDI Sotfware)

Resources for a beginner, professional, educator:

Books? _____

Catalogs? _____

Magazines?

_____

Contacts? _____ Demo's? _____

Other Suggestions/
Recommendations?_____

Notes:

MIDI CONNECTIONS

The following illustrations will show the basic connections used in the MIDI communications link. All MIDI equipment, interface hardware, thru boxes, and switches use the standard five pin MIDI port/cable connector.

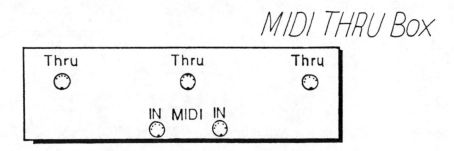

Figure 2.1

Five pin DIN MIDI cables used to connect MIDI devices

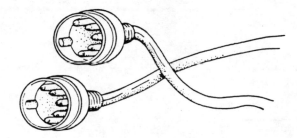

Figure 2.2

MIDI connection ports found on MIDI devices

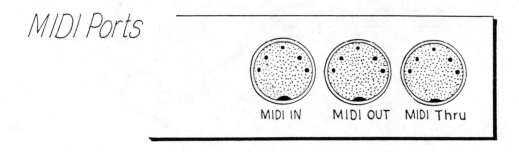

Figure 2.3

MIDI THRU Box is used to connect multiple MIDI devices instead of a daisy chain

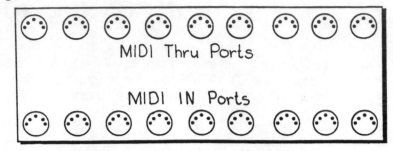

Switcher

MIDI Thru Ports

MIDI IN Ports

Figure 2.4

MIDI Switcher, like a MIDI THRU Box, connects additional MIDI devices

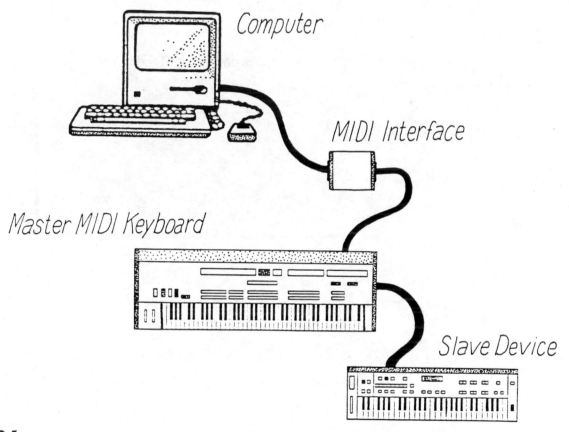

Computer

MIDI Interface

Master MIDI Keyboard

Slave Device

Figure 2.5

MIDI connection: Computer + MIDI interface + Master MIDI keyboard + Slave device

CHAPTER THREE
THE MUSICAL COMPUTER

The Apple IIGS Music System
Hardware And Equipment Planning
Guidelines For Setting Up The GS Music System
GS Music Software
Basic Operational And User Information

THE APPLE IIGS MUSIC SYSTEM

GS System Overveiw

When Apple Computer, Inc. developed the IIGS in1986, they added a new demension to personal computing: the ability to generate and playback digital sound through its own internal circuitry. The "G" stands for super high resolution graphics, and the "S" stands for digital sound ability. A standard IIGS system includes: the 65C816 microprocessor, internal 512K memory expandable to 8 Meg, clock and date, standard desk accessories, 80-column display, RGB analog monitor, background/border color options, built-in expansion slots, built-in ports for AppleTalk network, Imagewriter printer/ laser printer, mouse, and modem. Other features include a 4096 color palette ability, 15 voice sound chip, detached keyboard/number pad, numerous internal operating system options, RAM disk, sound adjustment, and disk drive options 3.5, 5.25, or a hard drive.

With the release of the new operating system (GS/OS), there will be a remarkable difference with the speed of the system. You should install GS/OS on all your GS software, but only the programs where the manufacturers have followed Apple's guidelines will be upgradeable.

GS Supportware

An important part of the Apple IIGS success record is its supportware: dedicated third-party developers of add-on hardware and remarkable software. Innovative manufacturers have designed expansion hardware cards to extend the GS sound capabilities. Several manufacturers have produced add-on stereo hardware for the GS. Any sound that passes through the sound chip is split into two channels for true stereo output. Also, several producers have marketed add-on digitizer cards to give you the ability to sample sound for programming use or for creating custom sound files, ASIF(Apple Standard Instrument File). The ASIF format can be loaded into most GS musical software programs for unique sound and customized instruments.

GS Sound

If you have heard the Apple IIGS playing music through external speakers, you have probably wondered how it was possible for a small computer to generate such quality sound. Without getting too technical, you should know a bit about how the GS can produce sound for music without using MIDI equipment. Every Apple IIGS has an incredible sound chip installed on its mother board called the Ensoniq Digital Oscillator Chip, or DOC, and Apple made sure that this sound chip can be addressed by special programmers' tools. The DOC can generate sounds by synthesis and electronically vibrate the diaphram of the IIGS speaker or recommended external speakers.

This powerful circuitry becomes the basis for emulating digital sounds for instruments, music, human voice, or any other sound saved in the ASIF format. But to actually create musical instrument sounds, the DOC must use waveforms to generate these digital sounds. The DOC has 32 oscillators used in15 pairs to form independent voices, while one pair remains reserved for internal use. Each voice, or pair, then uses a waveform as a guide to generate a specific sound effect. (Oscillator: Pulse-generating microelectronic circuitry in which the frequency that the pulse is generated will determine the tone.)

The GS music system has a predetermined-user market, and has been reserved for educational and home use, primarily, because the software digital instrument sound files vary in tone color quality. The GS sounds do not have high-end MIDI quality. In other words, the sound files cannot equal the sound generated by a deluxe Yamaha DX7 synth. However, the sound files do have very usable sound features and other options. For example, the GS has been used by professionals for quick sketching/composing of musical ideas and accompaniment sections in a composition. Most importantly, in an educational setting, the GS is a very powerful, motivational instuctional aid with every musical feature a teacher could imagine. Remember, the GS can also be interfaced with MIDI devices and become the center of a MIDI network by using sequencing software.

GS Sound Digitizing

The sound laboratory option consists of several add-on items. The SuperSonic Stereo Card splits the DOC's output to produce quality stereo results and can drive two external speakers. The Professional Digitizer reduces the hiss of the GS and gives you sound digitizing ability from an external source; a CD player works best. With the Professional Digitizer and Supersonic Stereo Card (FutureSound and Applied Engineering also have add-on card options), you will be able to digitize relatively clean recordings of an audio source into the computer's RAM (up to 8 MB). The digitized sounds will allow you to: create special effects (panning, mixing, fading), edit sound waveforms and save them onto disk, digitizer sounds and assign them to keys on the keyboard for real time control. You will need a quality 50 watt (minimum) stereo system and a CD player for the best results.

Sound digitizing is a great feature but it takes time and additional funds and still may not produce the sound quality you may desire. The sampling rate of the Professional Digitizer card and the all-in-one card by FutuerSound digitizer card is approximately 22 Kbytes per second. For a professional sample, approximately 44 Kbytes per second is used. Therefore, even though these digitizers work well, they still do not work well enough for professional sounding instrument files. If sound sampling is not an important goal for you, then just use the GS sound files contained within the music software. You may want to add digitizing abilities to your system at a later time, or move into MIDI or do both.

Other add-on hardware with similar but even less professional sound digitizing results are the MDIdeas Digitizer Card and the Sound Ace Audio Digitizer GS. These inexpensive add-on cards are an optional route to take with basic features for digitizer sounds into the GS for playback and experimental useand are excellent educational learning tools.

GS Advantage

One important advantage of using the Apple IIGS music system is that you can set it up and start using it in no time. You will have instant results as you begin to use and explore its musical abilities and applications. Musical ideas and possibilites become a reality through computer technology. The GS is a very user-friendly computer; the latest software features include: mouse interface, pull-down and up menu bars, understandable user-guides, good technical support from the manufacturers, and easy-to-learn and use software, great tool for illustrations—visual and audio. If you are interested in purchasing an Apple IIGS system to set up as a music system, you should first visit an authorized Apple dealer and judge the sound quality yourself.

GS Musicware

Music composition software designed for the IIGS is primarily "click-and-drag," meaning that musical notation is selected from a pull-up or pull-down menu bar and dragged to the grand staff by using a mouse or turbo mouse as an input device. This can be a time consuming task especially when composing a lenghty piece of music, but an excellent learning experience for reinforcing musical concepts and theories. GS software has a short learning curve and can almost be figured out without using the manual. Once the musical composition is in the computer, time-consuming tasks are quickly completed with a click of the mouse. Key and time signatures can be changed within seconds, Sections of accompaniment music can be created, copied, edited, and printed and practiced if desired. (See GS Music Software for more information.)

Other Software

There are many GS software packages with outstanding features that offer the user total control and ease of use in such applications as: word processing, page layout with laser print quality, paint and draw programs, business and education software, entertainment, creativity, telecommunications, as well as 90% compatibility with all existing Apple II software.

In additon, a new software package called Appleworks GS by Claris will add a whole new level of sophistication in integrated software. You can have six applications on screen at once, and open as many application windows as needed. Appleworks GS will take advantage of the speed, color graphics, and mouse interface of the IIGS. The six integrated programs will be loaded all at one time and there will be no need to re-boot the machine each time you want a new applications. Appleworks GS will include: Mac-like word processing with a built-in spellchecker and thesaurus, database, spreadsheet, page layout, paint/draw graphics, and telecommunications. One and a quarter MB of RAM will be needed to run this new software package; this amount of RAM should be purchased if you are planning to use the GS for serious production.

Summary

The Apple IIGS music system is an exciting, nonprofessional, easy-to-use musical toolbox that enables you to create, edit, and playback multi-timbral music from disk for illustration, drill work, composing, jamming, practicing, or even creating your own symphony! A MIDI interface, MIDI/GS software, and a MIDI keyboard allows you to enter music in real time.

HARDWARE AND EQUIPMENT PLANNING

Overview

You will want to plan and organize the setup of your Apple IIGS music system in a step-by-step fashion. The quality of the GS sound will be affected by the add-on, third-party products you purchase or choose not to purchase. But even these additional GS products may not produce the tone color or music system you desire.

First, you should become familiar with the standard 512K Apple IIGS system and what this package can do. Second, you should learn as much about the many upgrade/enhancement products that are available through Apple and third-party developers. (See Chapter Five: Product Information) Third, you should determine whether or not you will need all or some of the advanced features and enhancements for your intended musical use. Finally, determine how much of the musical GS system you will want to pursue.

Depending upon your budget, you may want to take full advantage of the "complete GS music system with sound digitizing ability and external audio equipment," or you can choose to organize "a basic GS music system" that will allow you to use the 512K GS, a few add-ons, and GS music software. Either the complete GS or the basic GS music system will produce fascinating sounds and the system will be user-friendly. One point to remember: if you have all the hardware, software, and audio equipment, you will eventually grow into these extras as you become more familiar with the system. Without any advanced features of the complete GS music system, you will not have the opportunity to explore and learn. A MIDI interface is always another option for even greater musical ability.

External Speaker Planning

If you already have a name brand integrated home stereo with 35-100 watts per channel and a pair of quality external speakers, this will be sufficient as well as a financial help. You will need one available auxiliary line in, in addition to the ones already used by your CD player, tape deck, or VCR/TV. Any one of these line outs can be converted into three additional line outs/standard RCA audio plugs by obtaining an "Audio System Connector" The connector is a switcher made by Sony, the SB-12 ($39) should be available at a local electronics store. It would be a good time to check all the existing wires and connections and do any repair/replacement that is needed.

The Bose RoomMate external speakers are a must if a stereo system is not availble when you plan out the organization of the basic Apple IIGS music system. The internal speaker of the GS will not provide ample output for your music applications. The Bose RoomMate external amplified speakers have been manufactured specifically for the GS. The Bose speakers have a 4.5 inch, full-range driver, an active equalizer, distortion limiting circuitry, and cost under $250. (See Chapter 5, *Product Information,* for less expensive, tight budget alternatives)

A quality stereo/amplifier and speaker system with an available auxiliary line out will usually provide the best sound for the GS music system, but plan on purchasing either the FutureSound's add-on stereo-digitizer card or the SuperSonic and ProDigitizer Cards for the best results. The hardware snap-in card also contain special DNR (Digital Noise Reduction) circuitry that has been designed for use with the GS. In addition, by using a stereo/amplifier, you can add bass and treble for an improved sound. If you have an equalizer, this adds another sound feature that you can use to manipulate the high, low, and midrange output.

Disk Drives and Printer Planning

A hard drive works best with the Apple IIGS because speed, storage, and software accessibility are important considerations. A SCSI card which is needed to interface with the hard drive will cost approximately $129. A non-Apple (20 MB) hard drive will cost approximately $500-700, depending upon the manufacturer. Two 3.5 floppy disk drives work well but have a "wait time" factor. One 3.5 floppy disk drive will cause too much switching of disks but certainly can be used if necessary.

A LaserWriter or compatible printer will produce higher quality print than a standard dot matrix printer. Cost for this ranges from $1,800-$5,500, depending on which laser printer you select (check NEC and Apple prices). The cost of a laser printer can be justified based on your intended use and future goals. A laser printer is faster and usually used with a professional MIDI system. The ImageWriter II or compatible printer produces a standard near letter quality print that is acceptable for home or educational use.

The Complete Apple IIGS Music System With Digitizing And MIDI Ability

The following list represents the equipment and accessories you will need to organize the complete Apple IIGS music system with special sound laboratory features. You will be able to use all GS music software, sample sound, create custom sound files with a CD player or any external audio source, and use powerful MIDI devices with MIDI sequencing software. You will need to see Chaper Five for purchasing suggestions and product descriptions.

•Apple IIGS with 512K (standard) and the GS/OS operating system software
•Apple 1.25 Meg expansion upgrade (MINIMUM)
•RGB analog monitor
•Keyboard and mouse/turbomouse*
•Two 3.5 disk drive or one 3.5 drive and a hard drive*
•External surge suppressor and cooling fan (Conserver or System Saver GS)
•Imagewriter or LaserWriter printer*
•FutureSound Stereo Card Digitizer Package or
•SuperSonic Stereo Card
•MDIdeas Professional Digitizer or basic Digitizer*
•MDIdeas Digitizer software or Professional Digitizer software
•One pair of Bose RoomMate speakers or
•A quality stereo amplifier with speakers (35 watt MINIMUM)
•CD player for sound sampling* (CD's with 4 times over sampling are superior quality)
•Ten blank formatted 3.5 disks (Double sided, double density)
•Several pairs of standard RCA sheilded cables
•Miscellaneous mini-stereo adapter jacks and plugs
•Apple MIDI interface or other Apple GS MIDI interface*
•MIDI synthesizer/sampler/drum machine*
•Several sets of standard MIDI cables*

GS Music Software
The Music Studio V2.0+, GS Music Construction Set+, Instant Music+ for nonmusicians, Pyware Music Writer and Music Administrator+, KidsTime II.+

-GS MIDI Software
The Music Studio 2.0+, GS Music Construction Set+, Personal Musician+, Master Tracks Jr+, Music Writer GS+, MusicPrinter 2.0, GlassTracks, Super Sequencer, ECL Music Training Programs+, MusicShapes+, and DIVERSI-TUNE+.

The Basic Apple IIGS Music System

The following list of items represent what you will need to organize the basic Apple IIGS music system. You will always be able to add-on sound digitizing and MIDI ability if your needs expand. The basic Apple IIGS music system will be appropriate for educational or home applications as you will be able to use all standard GS music software.

•Apple IIGS with 512K and the GS/OS operating system software
•RGB monitor
•Keyboard and mouse
•Surge surpressor strip
•Two 3.5 disk drives or one 3.5 disk drive and a hard drive*
•Imagewriter printer
•SuperSonic Stereo Card
•One pair of Bose RoomMate speakers
•Ten blank formated 3.5 disks
•GS music software (See Above for GS Software)

The * represents options.
The + sign represents recommended GS software.

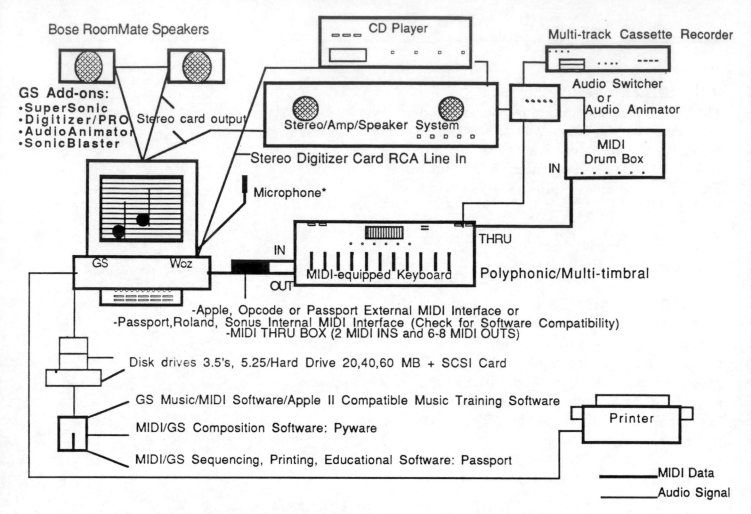

The Complete Apple IIGS/MIDI Configuration

•Musical electronic system for education or home.

•MIDI workstation with MIDI Interface, multi-timbral instrument, and MIDI drum box.

•Digitize sound--using add-ons + a microphone, CD, MIDI keyboard, or drum box.

•Stereo output for GS musical software with use of either external speakers.

•Use of external MIDI Interface with compatible MIDI software for sequencing and composition.

•MIDI/GS music printing and training software packages by Pyware

•MIDI output through stereo/amp. and speaker system.

•Management of custom sound files for GS software and MIDI instruments.

•Add-on potential for audio multi-track recorder and MIDI equipment.

•Sequencing software (MasterTracks Jr or Pro) for multi-track recording of MIDI instruments.

GUIDELINES FOR SETTING UP
THE GS MUSIC SYSTEM

Apple computer and each add-on hardware manufacturer will provide complete and detailed instructions for setup. The basic GS music system and the complete GS music system with sound digitizing features are relatively easy to understand and organize when you follow these instructions. The following information will provide additional guidelines and steps for helping you organize the Apple IIGS music system successfully.

Guidelines For The GS Music System

1. Most instruction manuals have been written for users with minimum technical experience and knowledge. Follow the Apple IIGS Owner's Guide thoroughly and any other product instruction manuals for installing and connecting the C.P.U., monitor, printer, floppy/hard drives, keyboard/mouse, expanded memory card/chips, etc. Run the self-diagnostic test to check the internal circuitry.

2. A surge supressor is a very important part of any computer system. Set up and use either the Conserver or the System Saver GS for proctection of your hardware, especially if you are planning to set up the complete GS music system. You should supress your audio equipment as well, or at least purchase a supressor strip to plug all your devices into.

3. Your GS music system will need a cooling fan when two or more add-on, internal hardware boards/cards are snapped into your GS expansion slots. A mono GS with just 512K will not need a fan. If you increase your RAM, add on a stereo card, and/or digitizer card, you must add cooling to the circuitry for protection as stipulated in the Apple IIGS guide. Either the Conserver by MDIdeas or the GS System Saver by Kensington are recommended for the Apple IIGS. Both units combine a cooling fan and supressor. The Conserver has more outlet plug-ins available than the System Saver. Note: Some Apple dealers have recommended not using the Apple manufactured GS internal cooling fan for musical applications; this fan adds additional GS noise to its circuitry.

4. You will need the Apple IIGS with 512K if you are planning to use just the basic music system. For extended use, however, you will have to expand the memory of the GS to range from 1.25MB to 8 MB. A GS with 1.25MB of RAM is desirable. If you purchase the Apple memory expansion card, its limit is1.25 MB. Other manufacturers (MDIdeas and Applied Engineering) offer upgrade boards that allow you to add chips as your needs expand. Usually, though, 1.25 MB will be sufficient to work with and run all software. Some hardware manufacturers utilize Apples' extended memory board and piggy-back their memory card to it to gain an additional eight MB. Note: When using 3.5 drives, keep in mind, long files should be saved as several different files for easy data management.

5. It is very important to fill out and send in all product warranty forms for your own protection, upgrades, repairs, and new product information.

6. Your 3.5 drives are the only drives you will need, unless you plan to run other Apple II software that uses 5.25 disk format. A hard drive is a very desirable piece of hardware for speed, storage, and data management. You will add-on a SCSI interface card for the hard drive. Once a hard drive is installed and initialized, you will copy all your software applications and files onto the hard drive and back up your data files regularly. For 3.5 drives, you will boot directly from them. Make sure you always back up your program disks and files using the Finder, GS/OS, or Copy II Plus.

7. Apple's Imagewriter II and Apple's laser printers should be used for best results. Most GS software has print drivers programmed for Apple printers. Connect your printer to the printer port on your GS.

8. Purchase and use hardware products from the leading developers, e.g., Apple, MDIdeas, Applied Engineering, and FutureSound and other recommended manufacturers found in this guide.

9. Most types of male and female plugs, cables, and adapters you will need are supplied with your hardware and equipment. You may need additional ones for your specific applications or equipment. Most every type of accessory is available from computer and electronic stores: Radio Shack, You-Do-It Electronics, and local Apple dealers, etc.

10. When you install specific GS add-on hardware, it is important for you to follow the manufacturers' installation instructions especially for the stereo card and digitizer card/s. In order to maximize the use of the GS expansion slots, you should follow these suggestions: Use Slot #2 for an internal optional MIDI interface card (e.g., PassPort interface), Slot #1 for the stereo/digitizer card, Slot# 6 for the Professional Dig-

itizer. The Modem Port or the Printer Port on the back panel of the GS can be used to connect the Apple's external MIDI interface box. An external modem (e.g. , Epic 2400 Plus) will also use the Modem Port; therefore, you may have to disconnect the devices if you choose external hardware devices. You will need only one MIDI interface—either an internal or an external device.

11. Pull the stereo card cables out the rear panel of the GS and connect your amplified speakers or connect the stereo card cables to an available auxiliary line out on your stereo using standard RCA cables. (See The Complete Apple IIGS/MIDI Configuration.)

12. Your digitizer cable should be connected to a CD player for best audio results. Pull this plug through the same or next panel opening on the rear of the GS and connect the digitizer line to the rear of your CD's audio IN. If a microphone came with your stereo card/digitizer follow the instructions.

13. Remember, the GS has the best of both worlds—slots and ports. Try to set up and utilize both the GS ports and slots for your convenience. The only time you will have to disconnect an external device is when you are sharing the same port, e.g., the printer port for the printer and Apple MIDI interface, or the modem port used for an external modem and the Apple MIDI interface and you should avoid this if possible. Usually, you will use the control panel (Open Apple, Control, ESC) and select which device you desire. You must reboot the GS to activate the selected slot/port. Note: Many GS users have an internal MIDI interface connected in Slot #2 and an external modem connected to the port, or an external MIDI interface and an internal modem. If you organizing your components in this way, you will avoid having to switch connections for various devices.

14. To connect a MIDI interface and keyboard to your GS, follow these suggestions: Decide whether you will use an internal or external MIDI device and what MIDI software packages will go with it. If you are using the Passport Design interface, you may have a problem pulling the head of the MIDI cable through the rear port hole of the GS. Some users have bent back the silver material around the port hole, on the rear panel, just enough to pull the MIDI cable through—*you may void your Apple warranty by doing this*. Another suggestion is to cut the MIDI cables and pull them through and re-solder the connections, and even others have just left the GS cover slightly loose and the MIDI cables left exposed.

15. You now know why Apple made an external MIDI interface box. To connect the Apple MIDI interface box just connect it to a selected port (printer or modem). Take your MIDI cables and plug them into your MIDI device.

16. A simple daisy chain using the MIDI THRU port on the rear panel of your MIDI device will connect a small MIDI network (two devices). If you plan to organize an extensive MIDI system, a MIDI THRU Box or MIDI switcher will be needed. Your MIDI software will coordinate your system.

17. Each MIDI device within your configuration will be connected by cables to another MIDI device: a master keyboard, interface, or MIDI THRU box switcher.

18. If you have questions, which you may, call your local Apple dealer first and then the specific manufacturers' technical support lines. The technicians know exactly what you are trying to do and the specifics of your questions. Don't guess! Your computer add-on boards and audio equipment are very sensitive; each installation step must be correctly.

GS MUSIC SOFTWARE

The following GS music software information will provide an easy-to-understand summary of the most popular programs available for the Apple IIGS music/MIDI system.

KIDS TIME II.
This program has been created for children aged three to ten, and has two educational programs emphasizing creativity, exploration, and skill development. KidsNotes allows a child to explore the many aspects of music and allows the user to create a song on a piano screen keyboard using a mouse. The second part of KIDS TIME II is called ABKEY. This program is a fun letter recognition/keyboard skill program with a variety of challenging levels. (Produced by Great Wave Software Co.)

MUSIC CONSTRUCTION SET GS.
This music composition program is a GS upgraded version from the award winning Music Construction Set. You compose music on the grand staff via mouse or MIDI keyboard. This program is an excellent tool for use in education as it represents a whole new world of computer-made music packed with fun and exciting sounds. (Produced by Electronic Arts)

THE MUSIC STUDIO V2.0.
This program is an educational and pre-professional music composition tool using standard musical notation with input via mouse or MIDI instrument. This premier GS music software contains powerful editing and play-ing features. Numerous files of digitized instrumental sounds are on disk and many other custom featurers. The GS program will plays up to fifteen instruments at once, prints, and contains a sound engineering laboratory screen, music paint box screen for children, and MIDI input options. (Produced by Activision/Mediagenic Inc.)

MUSICSHAPES.
A program to compose, record, and perform your own music in one sitting. This fun, easy-to-use software can be linked to the Apple GS Ensoniq Chip or a MIDI Casio CZ synthesizer. This nontraditional program has multi-sound capabilities that lets a novice, child, or a frustrated musician create exciting, original, four voice, multi-dimensional sounds and music. Musical shapes are used instead of standard musical notation. (Produced by MusicShapes.)

INSTANT MUSIC.
Through programmed artificial intelligence, this nontraditional music composition program is for music lovers with little or no music training. This program is a music creativity tool that uses up to four instruments and can play back music instantly. A unique jamming feature actually lets you play along using the mouse without hitting a bad note. This ingenious software is packed with outstanding features and is intended for the non-musician at home or school. This program allows the user to start creating music with electronic commands/tools. (Produced by Electronic Arts.)

JAM SESSION. (NEW RELEASE)

An Apple GS musical program for GS owners and nonmusicans. This music software will provide back-up music as you solo. The program allows the user to play any key on the computer keyboard without hitting a wrong note. This electronic music software for the GS lets the user experiment with a synthesizer. (Produced by Broderbund Software, Inc.)

DIVERSI-TUNE.

This powerful program is a 2-port, 32-channel in/out MIDI recorder, with overdub, punch-in/out audio editing, combining a 32-voice polyphonic, multi-timbral, stereo MIDI synthesizer, with an 88-key piano or bouncing ball. You can actually add words to any song, even songs on records, tapes, or CD's. Diversi-Tune can be used to make sing-a-long video tape for teaching songs in music classes. (Produced by Diversified Software Research, Inc.)

ESC MUSIC TRAINING PROGRAMS.

A complete family of music training products via MIDI. This series of music training programs include: Keyboard Tutor-MIDI, Early Music Skills-MIDI, Keyboard Extended Jazz Harmonies-MIDI, Keyboard Fingerings-MIDI, Keyboard Chords-MIDI, Keyboard Arpeggios-MIDI, Keyboard Speed Reading-MIDI, Musical Stairs-MIDI, Note Speller, Elements of Music, Music Flash Cards, Patterns and Pitch. (Produced by Electronic Courseware Inc.)

HOME STUDIO SYSTEM.

Create great home recordings with your GS, a sequencer/multi-track recording, editing, and graphics package. The Home Studio System includes: MasterTracks Jr and a Serial (External) MIDI Interface. (Produced by Passport Designs Inc.)

MASTER TRACKS JR.

This program is a GS designed package offering a professional and personal MIDI recording studio setting with all the powerful features found in professional quality MIDI software.

Since the Apple IIGS is still in the II family, the following list of powerful, professional Apple II software can also be used for MIDI musical applications:

-Master Tracks Pro Sequencer by PassPort Designs, Inc.

-Super Sequencer 128, GlassTracks, Personal Musician by Sonus Corp.

-MusicPrinter 2.0 by Temporal Acuity Products, Inc.

-Polywriter and Polywriter Utilities by PassPort Designs, Inc.

KEYBOARD BLUES-MIDI and KEYBOARD JAZZ HARMONIES-MIDI.

A program that teaches blues chords and includes drills and quizzes. Students can actually compose original blues solos with computer accompaniment. (Produced by Electronic Courseware Systems, Inc.)

MUSIC TUTOR-MIDI.

A three-part series program for ear training. It helps students hear and identify harmonies and chord structures and allows interaction both by the computer and the MIDI device. (Produced by PassPort Design.)

EAR TRAINING AND SIGHT SINGING.

A program in the Roland's Musicom Series that analyzes and identifies notes you sing into a microphone. It can identify single notes, intervals, and tunes and is designed to improve pitch recognition. (Produced by Roland Corp.)

MUSE (MIDI Users Sequencer/Editor)

A software package that allows you to create eight-track songs of up to 6000 notes each. A quality program that offers editing of measures and notes, transposition of tracks, and numerous other functions. (Produced by Roland

MASTERTRACKS PRO. (NEW RELEASE)

Professional sequencing for the GS with 16 multi-channel tracks. 240 clock beats per quarter note resolution, SMPTE format, save and open files in standard "MIDI file" fomat. Outstanding features in the Conductor Window, Song Editor, Makers Window and the Keyboard Mapper. (Produced by Passport Designs, Inc)

MUSIC ADMINISTRATOR.

The complete music office management system for the Apple IIGS. This program is fully interactiave, allowing you to mege and split information. You can produce comprehensive statistical, financial and student reports pre-designed in the system or design the type of report you desire. (Producedby Pyware)

MUSICWRITER. (Levels 1, 2, 3)
COMPOSING AND NOTATION

One of the few electronic music software printing programs developed just for the Apple IIGS. This is a music composition tool. It is easy enough for a beginner with no experience yet has all the power and utilities that a professional musician needs to create high quality music scores. Input music with a mouse or MIDI keyboard. Level 1 contains several tutorial files and a music theory guide, Level 2 and 3 offer professional composer, orchestra conductor or music director every feature desired. Compatible with the Imagewriter, Apple Laserwriter and Pyware MIDI Translator. (Produced by Pyware)

MIDI TRANSLATOR.

Convert MasterTracks Jr or a sequence file to a notation file for Pyware MusicWriter. This is a utility program that allows you to import a sequence file for the high quality print found in MusicWriter. Even though you can use a mouse or MIDI instrument with MusicWriter, some individuals still desire the use of a sequencer program for composing. This is a

highly recommended program for MT Jr, and MusicWriter. (Produced by Pyware)

INSTRUMENT DESIGNER.

You can create any instrument sound you wish. Alter sound waves, control sound attacks, sustans, decays, vibrators, pitch bends, and more. The program allows you to SEE and HEAR how modifications to sound waves effect sound. Pacth your synthesizer into your computer and let it drive the computer generated sounds. It also allows the user to create unlimited libraries of sound to be used with Pyware Music Writer. (Produced by Pyware)

HYPERSTUDIO. (NEW RELEASE)

Lets anyone create and use hypermedia applications. This is an amazing program. Combines Super Hi-Res graphics, text, and digitized sound files for any application as Hypercards are linked with buttons for easy use. This package includes: digitizer card, micrphone, amplified speaker and software. Possible applications are endless: interactive lessons, foreign language, customized student reports, and lots of fun too! (Produced by Roger Wagner)

BASIC OPERATIONAL AND USER INFORMATION

•The GS mouse, keyboard, trackball, MIDI devices, or previously composed/saved musical data on disk are the common input sources for musical data. You must know how to operate and use these devices and data files for music composition, editing, and sequencing.

•To create music and hear notes through the GS, you will use music software. Point and click the mouse button on the desired note from the parts box or pull-down/up menu bar and then drag it to the desired location on the musical staff and let go of the button. That specific note will be entered and then heard when you choose the "Played/Listen" command.

•The use of the menu commands helps to manipulate the musical data. The "Playback" commands will allow you to hear the sounds through the Bose RoomMate mini speaker system or an external amplifier and speaker system.

•To use and create music with the GS and a MIDI device, in real time, simple play the MIDI instrument. By using a MIDI interface, MIDI instrument, and MIDI software, your notes will appear on the screen and be played back and heard through the MIDI device's internal speakers or usually through external means. (Exernal amplifier and speaker system).

•Most music software has common pull-down commands via menu bar or standard keyboard strokes used to process musical data: Point, Click or Press the Command Key + a specific letter—"C" to copy, "X" to cut , "V" to paste, "S" to save, "P" to print, and variable commands for move, merge, punch in/out, sync, etc.

•Standard commands using a mouse/keyboard can change the volume, note duration, key, time signature, instrument files, song files, switch from GS sound to MIDI sound, and many other musical functions.

•When you save and record data, it should be stored on name brand disks and audio tapes. Back-up files should be maintained—a standard operating practice.

•In general, for beginners, the simpler the software application the more appeal and exchange. A computer with software that uses a mouse interface and/or MIDI devices usually produces more interaction with the individual and makes for a more stimulating learning experience.

•Playback and quality of sound and music should be through the Bose RoomMates or an external amplifier and speaker system.

•Some GS music software prints very slowly. For professional looking sheet music that is printed more quickly, a laser printer is recommended.

•When selecting a GS MIDI interface or any computer's interface, make sure MIDI data can be sent in and out and saved with specific software packages. For example, PassPort Designs' GS interface is MIDI out only and not

MIDI in when used with the Music Studio V2.0.

•The GS graphics and ease of use are attractive features and are powerful movtivators. The mouse interface and MIDI keyboard input are stimulating for creativity.

•If a high quality of print output is needed for sheet music/scores, all musical printing programs must have laser printer drivers preinstalled when you purchase the software. The laser printing option feature is usually found in the "Print Setup" section of the "File" menu. You should be able to choose among printers and quality of print as well.

•The GS "Playback" command will allow you to hear the musical data entered or stored. The quality of the tone color of the instrument sound, its volume level , and overall audio results, will depend on the audio means and the instrument sound files. (More than not, the GS is electronic sounding.)

•Common musical operations used in the GS music system include: the ability to add up to three verses of lyrics to a song, modify a file/song name, alter the specific components of an instrument sound's waveform (attack, decay, sustain, release), create endless files of customized instrument effects, turn off/on tracks of a multipart song for instrument practice, and use paintbox graphic symbols to free-form compose.

•Other musical functions and mouse commands allow you to: change quickly over to real time MIDI input/output/print, change key signature anywhere, change note stem direction, automatically insert measure bars, change note duration automatically, change volume and tempo at any time, and play multiple songs automatically.

•Even though most GS music composition programs are easy to use, reading the user manual, exploring time, and patience are simple elements to be observed. When you are learning a new software package, take the time to read the entire manual—from the front to rear. The user manual will help you know and understand the full range/features of the program. It has been discovered that many users only know 40-50% of the software's potential as they do not regularly refer to or have never read the manual.

CHAPTER FOUR
COMPUTER-BASED MIDI SYSTEMS

Getting Started: Organizing A Computer-MIDI System
Configurations: Computer-MIDI Systems
MIDI Basics: Understanding Tracks, Channels, And Sequencers
MIDI Lineups: Interfaces, Sequencing/Composition Software & Hardware

GETTING STARTED: ORGANIZING A COMPUTER-MIDI SYSTEM

Getting started with MIDI is exciting! You will soon discover the incredible synthesized sounds, control options, and uses for MIDI equipment. This section has been developed to start you off successfully, on your own MIDI journey, and to help you identify what you will need to make it—MIDI music! (For reference, see *Basic Configurations For Computer-MIDI Systems.*) These configurations have been provided to show several MIDI-user levels and how your system could be integrated. Each configuration represents a new level in music production ability. In addition, refer back to *MIDI Connections* for illustrations of basic MIDI equipment connections.

The operational commands for the many different software packages and MIDI products will be explained in detail by the manufacturers' user manuals. These user guides generally supply all the necessary support for operating a specific device. Commitment, practice, and patience will be important learning factors. Within a short time, you will have the computer controlling a MIDI device/s and you will soon learn the ins and outs of your system and computer software. You may eventually expand your system by installing additional MIDI gear and building an extensive MIDI configuration.

Identify The Basics

The following questions will help you identify some important start-up basics.

1. What level of music production do you wish to pursue? (MIDI-user levels can be classified into these three user categories: school or amateur use, pre-professional use, or professional performance and recording.)

2. What is the budget range for your MIDI system? Under $1000, between $2000 and $3000, $5000-$7000 or whatever it takes? Are you including or not including a computer?

3. What is your current hardware and equipment status? Do you presently have a computer and printer and do you want it to be the center of your MIDI system? Is there a MIDI interface and sequencing software available for your computer? Do you already have MIDI equipped instruments that can be wired in? And last of all, what quality audio equipment is presently accessible? (Amp? Pre-amp? Integrated amp/tuner? Quality speakers 50-100 watt rating? Cassette or multi-track recorder?)

Note: If you have an Apple II/compatible, Macintosh Plus, SE,II, IBM-PC/compatible, Commodare/Amiga, or Atari ST, these computers have plenty of MIDI support products.

MIDI Systems Components
Budget

Each MIDI-user level has its appropriate price tag. With a bit of consumer research and this guide, it is very conceivable that with no start-up equipment other than a home stereo system, you could organize and purchase a level one (school or amateur) MIDI system for under $3000. You may just find a computer-based MIDI system that should include: computer hardware (disk drives and dot matrix printer), MIDI software (sequencing and notation), internal/external MIDI interface, cables, as well as a low-end (priced) MIDI device. You may not be able to purchase top-of-the-line MIDI products like the New England Digital Synclavier, but it may be possible to purchase all pre-owned/outgrown equipment from a user group, computer society, modem/BBS MIDI forum, buyers' guide, or music store.

On the other hand, you may want to consider other brands of computers (MS-DOS) that are priced right for your budget, that could possibly have more RAM and speed. Remember, though, for a higher level of MIDI use some computers are just better for controlling MIDI data. You will find that many manufacturers of MIDI interfaces and software support a variety of computer systems.

The following budget amounts are only guidelines and prices change quarterly (microchips especially seem to fluctuate). The following MIDI-user levels will provide reasonable guidelines for accounting purposes, assuming that each level will need: a computer system and printer, MIDI software, MIDI equipment and audio equipment. (See Computer and MIDI Planning.)

Computer-MIDI system for school or amateur use—tight budget: $2950.
The system would consist of: A pre-owned enhanced Apple IIe or c computer with monitor, two disk drives ($1200) and an Epson printer ($350), a low-end Casio CZ101 ($300) or the new expandable Casio HT-700 MIDI synthesizer ($400, includes built-in speakers),

or another pre-owned MIDI polyphonic, multi-timbral synth, and the Passport MIDI Pac (MIDI interface IIe/c, Master Tracks, Polywriter, Polywriter Utility, sequencing, notation, printing software, $825-$875).

Computer-MIDI System for School or Amateur Use: $3,500-6,000.
(See *MIDI Lineups* for product recommendations; call for pricing)

Computer-MIDI System for Pre-Professional Use: $6,000-12,000.
(See *MIDI Lineups* for product recommendations; call for pricing)

Computer-MIDI System for Professional Performance: $10,000-20,0000+.
(See *MIDI Lineups* for product recommendations; call for pricing)

Professional MIDI Recording (Rent Recording Studio Time by the Hour)

Computer Hardware

As previously stated, the leading manufacturers of personal computers that can be connected to a MIDI system include, but are not limited to: Apple II and Macintosh, IBM's PC/XT, AT; Atari ST, Laser, and Commodores. If you own a personal computer, chances are it can be connected to a MIDI interface. Some musicians and professionals use leading computers right from the start. Budget permitting, it may be advisable to upgrade and just purchase a new personal computer with features similar to the ones listed under Chapter Two, *Helpful Guidelines and Buying Tips*.

Some personal computers have superior MIDI software support. The user-friendliness of the software is extremely important for most users including the pro's. Apple computers have been foremost in the early stages as well as in the current stages of the educational-professional MIDI market. Likewise, IBM and Atari ST series have very powerful music software and dedicated third-party developers supporting their use. The Atari ST line has convenient built-in MIDI ports, MIDI IN/OUT, ready for a MIDI cable and MIDI device.

MIDI Interface

One of the most important MIDI devices is the MIDI interface which enables your personal computer to communicate with your MIDI device/s. A MIDI interface is either a hardware card that is snapped into your computer's expansion slots, or if this is not possible, an external MIDI interface. The connection of your MIDI devices with your personal computer becomes an electronic music workstation.

MIDI interface hardware can range from $99-$199 for an Apple or Passport MIDI interface, with one MIDI IN and one MIDI OUT. Passport, Opcode or Sonus offer a variety of MIDI interfaces with tape and drum sync options or even a convenient THRU-Box (by Cooper) used for connecting a MIDI network. As previously mentioned, Atari ST's personal computers have built-in MIDI interface ports ready to be connected to a MIDI device. Many dealers/manufacturers offer packages: MIDI Interface + software that is intended for a specific application. If you plan to organize a MIDI system with several MIDI instruments, purchase a MIDI interface that is made for your computer and intended use. Some MIDI interface devices are equipped with several MIDI IN/OUT ports for connecting multiple devices.

MIDI Software

MIDI software is available in a variety of user levels and prices. You will need sequencing software to lay down tracks and to edit/control musical data, printing software to obtain sheet music, and composition software to compose and see notes on the screen. Some music software, like Deluxe Music Construction Set, allows the user to play in real time or even step time with a MIDI keyboard and mouse and includes a printing command which costs around $100.

Quality sequencing and music notation/printing software such as MASTER TRACKS PRO, FINALE, and Polywriter will range from $250 to $1000. (See Chapter Five for recommended software products.) It is very important to call the manufacturer and obtain a catalog and full product description for your intended use. Registered owners receive technical user support and upgrade information. Many dealers/manufacturers offer packages, namely, the MIDI interface + MIDI software.

If you are just starting out, purchase MIDI software with this point in mind: chances are you will eventually want to expand. (Call Coda, Passport, Sonus or Opcode for quality software suggestions.)

MIDI Devices

Don't guess! A MIDI compatible device is labeled "MIDI" right on the rear of the case. Many keyboards and electronic instruments on the market today are not MIDI. They may have great sound abilities, user-features, and deserve merit, but still are not MIDI. If in doubt, look at the rear panel of the equipment and find the MIDI ports. The MIDI ports will be clearly labeled. The MIDI-IN/OUT/THRU ports will look like two or three small, round receptacles, a bit smaller than a dime, with five DIN holes ready to receive the male MIDI plug that has five DIN pins.

Standard commercial MIDI devices and related audio equipment include: MIDI synthesizers, samplers (keyboard and module unit), rhythm drum machines, MIDI controllers, MIDI sequencing hardware, MIDI filters, MIDI mixers, MIDI sync boxes, wind-to-MIDI devices (saxosynth), signal processors, mixdown boards, SMPTE devices, MIDI patch bays, MIDI switchers, MIDI channelizers, and even MIDI lighting controllers. A MIDI-THRU Box allows anywhere from two MIDI INs to four, six or eight MIDI OUTs.

Note: MIDI designs and configurations are commonly set up without a computer. Sequencing hardware controls and coordinates the MIDI configuration thus replacing the computer and sequencing software.

Common features and standards relating to MIDI devices include: Digital and analog based circuitry, usually electronic not electric, polyphonic and monophonic, MIDI ports labeled "IN/OUT/THRU or MIDI IN/OUT," synthesizer keyboards and modules or rack units, sampling keyboards and modules or rack units, with and without waveform editing ability, play only, internal RAM-cartridge/floppy-disk drive for voice librarians. Some MIDI keyboards are even equipped with a drum machine, a built-in sequencer and signal processor. The Korg M1, Roland D-20, and the Ensoniq SQ-80 are new, all-in-one MIDI workstations.

Just when you purchase your new MIDI devices (synthesizer, sampler, drum machine, signal processors) new product lines continue to be announced quarterly. An option to consider when purchasing MIDI equipment or top-of-the-line equipment, is to find a music dealer/store that will allow trade-ins and trade-ups—a definite possibility for an individual who experiments with devices and desires to upgrade the system frequently.

Unfortunately, you will probably experience a 50% or greater loss for trading in your MIDI equipment. Or, you may wish to keep these devices to build a MIDI configuration using your older equipment as slave devices. Usually a MIDI configuration will consist of one high-quality synth/sampler and several of these older devices.

A feature-rich, top-of-the line synth or sampler keyboard will range from $1000-$2000. Some keyboards priced around the $1000 range are equipped with rich, fat sounds but only contain pre-sets and are not programmable. Other keyboards with a higher price tag include pre-sets that are programmable with every imaginable function. It is usually a good idea for a beginner to read about and generally understand the fundamentals of synthesized sound. MIDI keyboard-synthesizers are very complex and it is possible for a new user to "over purchase" and acquire a synth that may be too advanced and difficult to fully understand.

A common path to take is to purchase easier-to-use MIDI equipment at first and then grow into more sophisticated and expensive units. The advanced series of Yamaha DX, Roland, Korg, and Ensoniq synthesizers and sampler keyboards are full-function musical instruments with champion features. These advanced series are a tough place to start and are not usually recommended for the beginner—but mastering them should be a goal for any serious user. The Casio CZ and HT MIDI line of synthesizer keyboards is one of the most popular lines for beginners and students.

Printer

Using a printer with a computer-MIDI system is simple. The software will contain a print command. You will use either a dot matrix printer that will give you a slow printout of fair to good quality, or a laser printer that will be quick and provide a high-grade print of sheet music. A dot matrix printer can be purchased for as low as $300 and a laser printer can be found for as low as $1,800 (e.g., the NEC laser printer lines). If you intend to use a laser printer, check to see if your MIDI software is laser-compatible.

Audio Equipment

If you are organizing your computer-MIDI system on a tight budget, the average home stereo can be used for a school or amateur MIDI system if necessary. Some miscellaneous RCA cables, stereo jacks, MIDI cables, and low pass filtering may be needed. In addition, if you intend to produce recordings, a mixer and multi-track recorder are important audio components. These audio devices are used for recording, controlling, and separating the tracks. You should consider the quality of sound, the amount of power you need, and the amount of wattage of your speakers.

A wide variety of audio accessories are available and can be used in your MIDI configuration: multiple amps, reverb units, digital delays, graphic EQ's, and patch bay connectors. Each sound quality you are searching for will have a price.

For pre-professional or professional recording, only name brand studio-quality amplifiers/pre-amps, mixers, mixdown decks, multitrack recorders, speakers and other recording high-end audio equipment must be used to capture quality sound. A professional MIDI recording studio will provide the best results. See Chapter Six, *Resources For Purchasing and Development* for MIDI related periodical and professional recording literature.

Connecting MIDI Devices

All MIDI connections use a special five pin DIN, MIDI plug and receptacle. Follow all recommended manufacturers' guidelines for connecting your specific MIDI gear. When three or more devices are connected, use a MIDI THRU device as timing glitches in the entire MIDI system can occur.

Note: Surge suppress all your equipment against AC voltage spikes and brownouts.

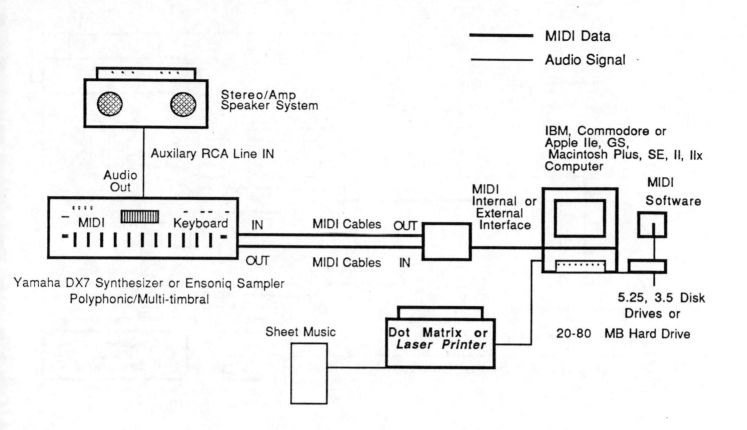

Music Composition and Printing Workstation

•Personal computer with one MB of Ram, Laser Printer or Dot Matrix Printer.

•Sequencing, Notation Software by: Passport, Pyware, Sonus, Coda, Opcode, etc.

•Apple, Opcode, Passport, or Sonus MIDI interface (Internal/External).

•Yamaha, Ensoniq, Korg, Casio or other MIDI keyboard/devices.

•Expansion options for additional MIDI devices using MIDI Thru Box.

•Optional SMPTE and Multi-track Cassett Recording.

Configuration 4.1 Computer MIDI-System

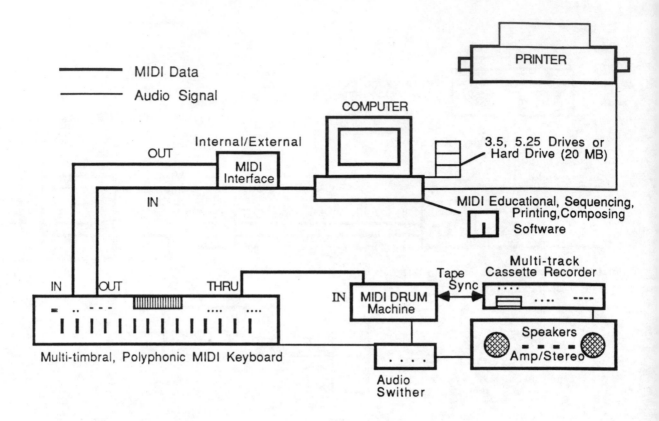

MIDI Daisy Chain: Keyboard and Drum Machine

•Personal Computer with RAM upgrade.

•Standard MIDI interface from: Passport, Roland, Sonus, or Opcode.

•MIDI keyboard, synthesizer or sampler with MIDI THRU.

•Programmable MIDI drum machine.

•MIDI Sequencing, Notation, and Educational software.

•Simple daisy chain setup using MIDI THRU.

•Option for Tape and Drum sync recording.

Configuration 4.2 Computer-MIDI System

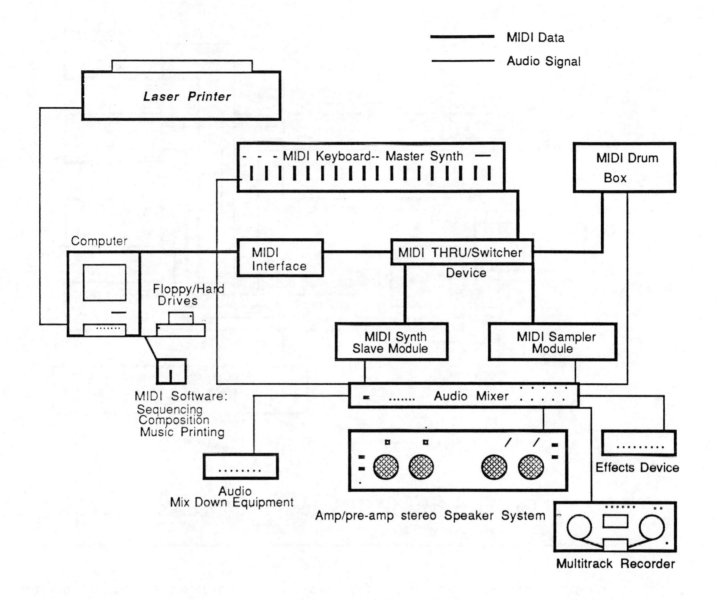

Computer-based MIDI Recording/Workstation (A)

- Personal computer with minimum 1.25 MB RAM, external storage, and laser printer.

- Standard MIDI interface THRU box or Switcher for multiple MIDI instruments.

- MIDI software for sequencing, composition, voice librarians, and patch editing.

- Audio equipment for effects, mixing, and multitrack recording.

- Drum box/tape sync recording with options for add-ons: Merge box, SMPTE, recording.

Configuration 4.3 Computer-MIDI Systems

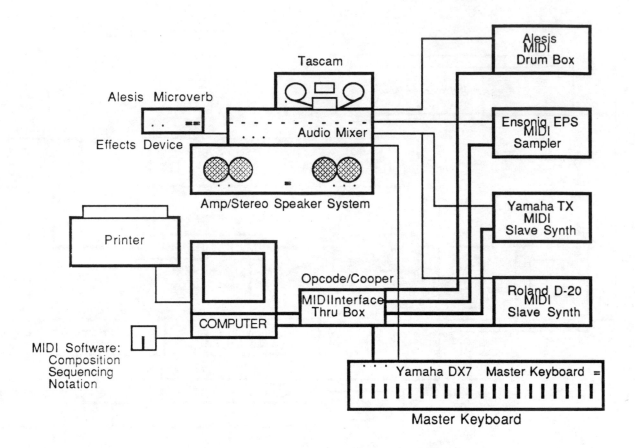

Computer-based MIDI Recording/Workstation (B)

•Computer with (1.25 MB of RAM,check for system requirements) two drives or hard drive.

•Standard MIDI interface THRU box or Switcher for multiple MIDI instruments.

•MIDI software for sequencing, composition, voice librarians, and patch editing, etc.

•Audio equipment for effects, mixing, and multitrack recording.

•Drum box/tape sync recording with options for add-ons: Merge box and SMPTE, recording.

Configuration 4.4 Computer MIDI System

MIDI BASICS:
UNDERSTANDING CHANNELS,
TRACKS & SEQUENCERS

MIDI Channels

The MIDI communication standard has been developed to allow for 16 channels of musical data to be transmitted IN/OUT/THRU your MIDI cables to your MIDI device/s and computer. These assignable MIDI channels will transmit a variety of digital information such as: what notes are being played on your polyphonic/ multitimbral keyboard (note on/off), with what degree of touch-release sensitivity, the velocity sensing, and even sound patch switching within your MIDI device, as well as what control levers and pedals are used to regulate the pitch, timbre, vibrato and volume.

You could, for example, assign channel one to a MIDI instrument that contains a tight brass sound, a second channel to a drum machine with a pre-programmed rhythm, and a third channel to a slave synth or module, set for any one of its many patches or presets playing the melody lead. Remember, multitimbral MIDI devices can be assigned more than one tone color and channel. You could continue to build an entire composition around three MIDI devices assigning each instrument different channels and multi-parts and voices.

Also, MIDI devices are equipped with LCD display screens and buttons to control and set channels. The instrument's control features regulate waveforms, values, tone colors, parameters, vibrato, delay, tone mix, pitch, the selected waveform envelope to be altered, and the octave. Your computer, sequencer, and MIDI devices will, literally, conduct the whole operation once you have assigned the parts.

Tracks

Sequencer hardware and sequencing software are like digital tape recorders that contain data tracks (4, 8, 12, 16, 24, 32, 64...256 to an unlimited amount) that can direct and store musical data. For starters, the use of tracks on a MIDI sequencer will allow you to organize, create, compose, assign octaves, instruments, and sound patches within the MIDI configuration.

Tracks in a sequencer will be designated to a specific MIDI channel as each numbered track can play and store specific instrument parts. Multiple tracks can be programmed to the same MIDI channel of the same device or any MIDI device within the design.

Sequencers

Sequencers accumulate and coordinate musical data for each component's parts, much in the same way as a conductor of an orchestra. The sequencer will allow each device to perform as part of an ensemble. Sequencers primarily store data in much the same way as a multi-track recorder with powerful editing and storing ability. There are three forms of sequencers: a computer + sequencing software, a stand-alone MIDI sequencing device (equipped with a LCD display screen) or a MIDI keyboard equipped with a built-in sequencer. Sequencing software has advantages over hardware; namely, the wider computer screen, easy upgrades, ease of use, and more workability for separation and assignments. Some software sequencers include a printing command or would use a utility program to obtain printed sheet music.

Note: The software sequencer will be limited to the capacity of your computer's memory: 128K, 512K, 1MB- 8MB/external storage.

Your sequencer, software or hardware, will have a user manual to guide you through the basic operations. When sequencing musical data via software, it can be entered by real time or step time thus giving you more control and operational options.

Broadly speaking, sequencers should have the following features and operational commands:

•Assign any one of the sequencing tracks to any one of the16 channels
•Perform auto-correct/quantization
•Contain punch in/out and auto punch functions
•Regulate tempo changes and transpose key signatures
•Program all changes and create file names
•Perform forward/reverse/search commands
•Incorporate a variety of filtering options
•Convert real-time sequencing to step-time files
•Execute screen editing by using cut, copy, paste functions

•Song mode to step sequencing and master clock
•Control system exclusive data

Each level of software sequencers contain advanced features and use more computer memory.

MIDI Interface Listings, Sequencing and Composition Software, and MIDI Hardware Recommendations

(All manufacturers should be contacted directly for product information and for new product.)

Computer Type	MIDI Interface/s	Sequencing and Music Composition Software	MIDI Hardware/Keyboards,Synths,Drum Machine, etc.
Apple MAC Plus	-Apple MIDI Interface	Deluxe Music Construction Set V. 2.0	AKAI S900, MK 73 Controller Casio CZ101 or HT-700, FZ-1, 3000 Ensoniq ESQ-1 Ensoniq EPS Performance Sampler Ensoniq Mirage Digital Multi-Sampler DSK Fostex Multi-Track Recorder
Apple MAC SE	-Opcode Professional Plus -Opcode Studio Plus	"M" V. 1.0 Opcode Sequencer 2.5	
Apple MAC II and IIX	-Opcode Time Code Machine	Jam Factory V 1.0 UpBeat	Kawai K1
	-Passport MIDI Interface -Passport MIDI Transport	Finale	Korg SGX-1, 1D and M1 Series Korg DS and DW Series Additional MIDI cables for each MIDI device
		Performer V. 2.0 Professional Composer Opcode Music Mouse Opcode Oval Tune Opcode Strawberry Oval Tune (Mac II)	Oberheim Matrix 6/6R Oberheim Xpander/Matrix 12
	-Sonus MacFace MIDI -SMX 2000SMPTE/MIDI Sync -MDM 80 MIDI-FSK Sync	Passport Master Tracks Pro Masterpiece Superscore MIDI Paint	Roland D-20 Roland and Juno and Super Juno Roland Alpha Juno 1 & 2 Roland RD Piano Series
		Educational: Listen, 7th Heaven Music Mouse	TASCAM Multi-Track Recorder Technics SX-PR60 Yamaha DX7, TX, and DSR Series
			Digital Music Corp. MIDI Patch Bay/Processor Drum Machines: Alesis Drum Machine Korg DDD Series Roland TR Series (505) Simmons Drum Series
			MIDI THRU-Box: Cooper Box
Apple II+, e, GS	Passport MIDI Interface -GS Serial External MIDI Interface -w/Interface and Drum Sync -w/Interface and Tape/Drum -IIe Internal MIDI card	Master Tracks II+, e, GS Master Tracks Pro IIe (Enhanced) Master Tack Jr. & PRO for GS	(Use with multiple Korg KMT MIDI devies) Sonus MT Opcode Studio Plus II
			Outboard Effects: Alesis Microveb
Apple IIe	Apple MIDI Interface (GS)	MIDI 8 Plus IIe, GS MIDI 4 Plus IIe, Polywriter IIe, GS Pyware: MIDI Composition System	Professional and Educational
Apple IIGS	Opcode GS Professional Plus GS Studio Plus Two	Glass Tracks IIe, GS Super Sequencer IIe, GS	Computer-MIDI System Recommendation:
			A. Apple Macintosh Plus/SE, II Computer Extra Opcode Studio Plus II Interface Drive or Mastertrack Pro Sequencer Hard Drive Your MIDI Devices
	Sonus IIe Interface	Music Printer V. 2.0	B. Apple Macintosh Plus/SE, II Computer Extra Opcode Studio Plus II, Three Drive or MasterTracks Pro Sequencer Hard Drive Visions Sequencer Your MIDI Devices
		Music Construction Set GS The Music Studio V. 2.0 Music Shapes Instant Music GS Diversi-Tune	C. Apple IIe, GS Computer Two Drives Passport MIDI Interface Hard Drive Mastertrack Pro or Jr. MIDI Translator MIDI-Thru Box Pyware Music Writer (Levels 1,2,3) Your MIDI Devices

NOTE: The length of time you can record in "real time" using Apple II sequencing and composition software varies in minutes.

Always check with the mfg. to get the real time recording length..."How much memory of the computer can you use?"

CHAPTER FIVE
PRODUCT INFORMATION

GS Software
Apple II Music And MIDI Software
Software Resources For Electronic Music Education
Macintosh Software
Apple II And GS Hardware
Macintosh MIDI Hardware

PRODUCT INFORMATION

The following listings of software and hardware products have been compiled for educators, music professionals, and amatuer users. This resource represents many of the leading support products that are available for musical electronics. Call the manufacturer for detailed information and for clarification. *Telephone numbers may be subject to change without notice.*

APPLE IIGS SOFTWARE.

DIVERSI-TUNE.
A utility music writer and tool. A powerful computer program designed for educators, computer enthusiasts, and musicians for use as a music tool. This program has three basic functions: Sound synthesizer, screen display for editing, and a MIDI music recorder. Use MIDI or the GS' sound ability. Diversified Software Research, Inc., 34880 Bunker Hill, Farmington, MI 48331-3236, 1-800-835-2246 ext. 127, orders only. For information call 313-553-9460. $55.

MASTER TRACKS.
Professional MIDI power. A powerful MIDI sequencing program offering professional MIDI recording and editing available for the Apple IIGS. Use real-time, step-time and song mode sequencing of up to 2 Meg of expanded memory. The program utilizes a sequencer and song mode for sending and receiving MIDI data. In addition it can can sync to song and/or videotape. Apple IIe, c, GS) Passport Designs, Inc., 625 Miramontes St., Suite103, Half Moon Bay, CA 94109, 414-726-0280. $249.95.

MASTER TRACKS JR.
Easier to use MIDI recording software for music composition and editing with 64-tracks for recording, punch in/out, graphic song editor, step record mode, as well as a variety of other powerful featurers. Passport Designs, 625 Miramontes Street, Suite 103, Half Moon Bay, CA 94019, 415-726-0280.

MUSIC CONSTRUCTION SET.
Point, click, and compose. This GS version of Music Construction Set has been enhanced with special digitized sound instrument files, like the grand panio. By using the mouse or a MIDI keyboard, you can compose, play, and print music. Electronic Arts, 1820 Gateway Dr., San Mateo, CA 94404, 415-571-7171. A stereo card and speakers are recommeded for higher quality output. $49.95.

MUSICSHAPES.
Music composition with graphics. By using two screens, fascinating melodic sound patterns can be arranged to compose music. This educational or home package is a fascinating way to teach and learn about traditional music in a nontraditional method.

Mouse or MIDI input will allow the user to explore sound and musical concepts in a fun and entertaining style. Music Systems for Learning, Inc., 311 E. 38th St., Suite 20C, New York, NY 10016, 212-661-6096. $175.

PYWARE MUSIC WRITER.
Professional musicians software. This music composition tool utilizes the DOC fully. A complete selection of musical notation symbols for serious composition. $295 Pyware Music Writer, special edition $595 retail, Pyware Music Writer, professional model, call for details. See below for address.

PYWARE MUSIC ADMINISTRATOR.
A music educator's accounting tool. This GS program will keep records for just about any need a music teacher has: students' information/files, a music data library, uniform data, and even department inventory records as well as a general ledger and more. Pygraphics Corp., P.O. Box 639, Grapevine, TX 7605. Call 800-222-7536 or 817-481-7536. for details. $295.

ECL MUSIC TRAINING PROGRAMS.
Complete set of educational training software. This family of music training products for the Apple IIGS utilizes a MIDI interface card and a synthesizer. This educational package (each sold separtely) consists of thirteen individual programs. Electronic Courseware Systems, Inc., 1210 Lancaster Dr., Champaign, IL 61821. Call: 217-359-7099 for details. $39.95-99.95.

THE MUSIC STUDIO V2.0.
Three music/sound programs in one. Point, click, and pull down menus for composing music using standard music notation symbols, or use a MIDI interface and synthesizer for input. A paint-style section of this program changes musical notation into colors and shapes for free-style composition. The sound editor section allows the user to customize a specific sound envelope. The Music Studio was one of the first programs designed for the GS and the new version V2.0 offers many more features and powerful file/sound management via sound digitizing. Mediagenic/Activision, 2350 Bayshore Parkway, PO Box 7286, Mountain View, CA 94039, 415-960-0410. $79.95.

INSTANT MUSIC.
Get down and jam. A fascinating music composition program for all GS owners and nonmusicians. There are four instruments that can be played at the same time through the Apple GS Bose RoomMate speakers or through a GS connected to a home stereo. The user sees small rectangular shapes on the screen which represents standard musical notation. Take control of the mouse and jam along or create your own music through artificial intelligence. There are also two additional data disks available with many digitized instruments and songs. Electronic Arts, 1820 Gateway Dr., San Mateo, CA 94404, 414-571-7171. $49.95. New sound and song files include: "It's Only Rock 'N Roll" and for "Hot & Cool Jazz. $29.95 each.

JAM SESSION.
An Apple GS musical program for GS owners and nonmusicans. This music software will provide back-up music as you solo. The program allows the user to play any key on the computer keyboard without hitting a wrong note. This electronic music software for the GS lets the user experiment

with a synthesizer. Broderbund Software, Inc. 17 Paul Drive, San Rafael, CA 94903-2101. Orders: 800-527-6263; by mail: Broderbund Software-Direct, P.O. Box 12947, San Rafael, CA 94913.

GS MUSIC FILES.
Beethoven, Beatles, Broadway, theme songs, classical, rock, jazz, TV theme songs. GS music files are available for GS Music Construction Set and GS Music Studio. Product identification numbers are: GS10, GS13, GS20, GS21 music files, $9 each. Orders: 800-331-8125, CA 408-496-0624. Public Domain Exchange, 2074C Walsh Avenue, #763, Santa Clara, CA 95050.

KIDSTIME II.
An educational package for young children. A super program for the GS and children that emphasizes creativity, exploration, and skill development. KidsTime II contains two educational programs: ABKey and KidsNotes. Great Wave Software, 5353 Scotts Valley Dr., Scotts Valley, CA 95066, 408-438-1990. $39.95.

APPLE II MUSIC AND MIDI SOFTWARE.

(Several software listings include only the product's name—this has been done to ensure manufacturer/dealer contact for full product information as well as Apple IIe, c and GS compatibility; check for RAM requirements.)

MUSIC WRITER FOR IIe.
MIDI input and music printing/composition program. Pygraphics, PO Box 639, Grapevine, TX 76051, 817-481-7536 or 800-222-7536. Level 1, $295, Level 2, $595. Call for details.

MUSIC WRITER FOR THE IIGS.
MIDI/mouse input and music printing/composition program: Levels 1-3 $295-595. Pygraphics, PO Box 639, Grapevine, TX 76051, 817-481-7536 or 800-222-7536.

GLASSTRACKS.
Professional MIDI recording software. Sonus Corporation, 21430 Strathern Street, Suite H, Canoga Park, CA 91304, 818-702-0992. Call for pricing and product information..

MIDI/8 PLUS.
Eight channel multi-track recording software. A professional recording studio with unlimited overdubbing to create up to eight independent parts assignable on any MIDI channel with professional features such as: punch in/out, auto correct, looping, tape or drum sync, linking and much more! Passport Designs, 625 Miramontes St., Half Moon Bay, CA 94109, 415-726-0280. Apple II's, GS, and Commodore, $149.95.

POLYWRITER.
Transcription MIDI software. Real-time input, and automatic transcription to create a score in a variety of formats. Passport Designs, 625 Miramontes St., Half Moon Bay, CA 94109, 415-726-0280. Apple II plus, Apple IIe, Apple IIc, Apple IIGS. $299.95.

MIDI VOICE LIBRARIAN.
MIDI sound librarian. Amazing sound files for your Casio CZ Series, Yamaha DX-7, Roland JX-8P, Roland Juno 106 and Oberheim OB-8 keyboards. Passport Designs; 625 Miramontes St., Half Moon Bay, CA 9410, 415-726-0280. $69.95.

PASSPORT MIDI VOICE EDITOR.
A voice librarian editor for the Yamaha FB-01. Organize, edit, manage, and manipulate configurations and sounds for the Yamaha FB-01 synthesizer/module. Passport Designs, 625 Miramontes St., Half Moon Bay, CA 94109, 415-726-0280. Apple IIe, GS. $125.00.

MUSIC TUTOR-MIDI.
Passport Designs, 625 Miramontes Street; Suite 103, Half Moon Bay, CA 94019; 415-726-0280. Call for details.

AURAL SKILLS TRAINER.
Electronic Courseware Systems Inc., 1210 Lancaster Dr., Champaign, IL 61821, 217-359-7099. $99.95 per set, $39.95 per disk.

KEYBOARD BLUES-MIDI.
Electronic Courseware Systems Inc., 1210 Lancaster Dr., Champaign, IL 61821, 217-359-7099. $79.95.

KEYBOARD JAZZ HARMONIES-MIDI.
Electronic Courseware Systems Inc., 1210 Lancaster Dr., Champaign, IL 61821, 217-359-7099. $79.95.

MICROBAND.
Electronic Courseware Systems Inc., 1210 Lancaster Dr., Champaign, IL 61821, 217-359-7099. $79.95

FINGERING SERIES.
Wenger Corporation Learning Division, 1401 East 79th Street, Bloomington, MN 55420, 612-854-9554. (Woodwind or brass series), $99, $29 per program.

MUSIC CLASS SERIES.
(Fundamentals, Rhythm, Ear Training, Music Symbols, Note Reading). Wenger Corporation Learning Division, 1401 East 79th Street, Bloomington, MN 55420, 612-854-9554.

NOTE US.
Educational software for sight reading and learning. Computers and ME, 10 Ashbrook Road, Exeter, NH 03833. Call 603-772-8850 for complete product details.

MASTER TRACKS.
Professional MIDI power. A powerful MIDI sequencing program offering professional MIDI recording and editing available for the Apple IIGS. Use real-time, step-time and song mode sequencing of up to 2 Meg of expanded memory. The program utilizes a sequencer and song mode for sending and receiving MIDI data. In addition it can sync to song and/or videotape. Apple IIe, c, GS. Passport Designs, Inc., 625 Miramontes St., 103, Half Moon Bay, CA 94109, 414-726-0280. $249.95.

MASTER TRACKS PRO.
A professional MIDI recording and editing program with such features as: 64 tracks of real-time/step-time input, graphic song editing, a librarian and easy-to-use tape controls for punch in/out, graphic step and MIDI data editing as well as numerous MIDI features for film and video soundtracks. Passport Designs, 625 Miramontes Street, Suite 103, Half Moon Bay, CA 94019, 415-726-0280. $299.95.

POLYWRITER.
See above for description. Passport Designs, 625 Miramontes Street, Suite 103, Half Moon Bay, CA 94019, 415-726-0280. $299.95

MUSE.
Roland Corp U.S., 7200 Dominion Circle, Los Angeles, CA 90040, 212-685-5141. $150.

MUSICOM SERIES.
Roland Corp U.S., 7200 Dominion Circle, Los Angeles, CA 90040, 212-685-5141. $425.

PERSONAL MUSICIAN.
Sonus, 21430 Strathern Street, Suite H, Canoga Park, CA 91304, 818-702-0992. $129.95.

SUPER SEQUENCER.
Sonus, 21430 Strathern Street, Suite H, Canoga Park, CA 91304, 818-702-0992. $275.95.

SOFTWARE RESOURCES FOR MUSIC EDUCATION.

ADVANCED SOFTWARE.
18520 Vincennes #31, Northridge, CA 91324. Call 818-349-9334 for complete music software details/pitch to MIDI.

ELECTRONIC COURSEWARE SYSTEMS.
1210 Lancaster Drive, Champaign, IL 61821. For complete information about 250 instructional music software packages for most every name of computer, call 217-359-7099.

HYBRID ARTS, INC.
11920 West Olympic Blvd., Los Angeles, CA 90064. Call 213-826-3777 for Atari ST music software; scoring and sequencing packages.

MIMETICS CORPORATION.
PO Box 1560, Cupertino, CA 95015. Call 408-741-0117 for MIDI interface and music sequencing software for Commodore Amiga computers.

MIX BOOKSHELF.
6400 Hollis Street, Suite #12, Emeryville, CA 94608. Call 800-233-9604 or 415-653-3307 for top-of-the software and educational, professional and high-tech tools for the audio/video/music recording industries.

TEMPORAL ACUITY PRODUCTS.
300 120th Avenue NE, Building #1, Bellevue, WA 98005. Call 206-462-1007 for complete details about Apple and MS-DOS educational software for ear training, sight reading, music printing, composition, and theory.

VOYETRA TECHNOLOGIES.
Dept. K, 333 Fifth Avenue, Pelham, NY 10803. Send for details for IBM PC/AT and compatible sequencing music software.

MACINTOSH SOFTWARE.

FINALE.
Professional music printing and more! With Finale, you just sit at your MIDI keyboard and improvise your score using expressive dynamics and rubato. Within seconds, your score will appear on the screen in standard music notation. Finale even has its own PostScript font called Petrucci. You can also customize and create symbols to fit any

publisher's requirements. Call 1-800-843-1337, collect 612-854-9554 for the nearest dealer; or call CODA. $1000.

MASTER TRACKS PRO 3.0.

A professional MIDI recording and editing program with such features as: 64 tracks of real-time/step-time input, graphic song editing, a system exclusive librarian and easy-to-use tape recorder style controls for punch in/out, graphic step and MIDI data editing as well as numerous MIDI features for film and video soundtracks. Passport Designs, 625 Miramontes Street, Suite 103, Half Moon Bay, CA 94019, 415-726-0280.

MASTER TRACKS JR.

Easier to use MIDI recording software for music composition and editing with 64-tracks for recording, punch in/out, graphic song editor, step record mode, as well as a variety of other powerful features. Passport Designs, 625 Miramontes Street, Suite 103, Half Moon Bay, CA 94019, 415-726-0280.

KEYBOARD VIRTUOSO.

IMPROVISATIONAL ARTS: Americana, Mardi Gras Jazz, Dixieland Jazz, Boogie Woogie, Swing, MIDI Jazz, Bluesology. TRADITIONAL PIANO: Concert Piano level 1, Concert Piano level 2, Concert Piano level 3, Concert Favorites #1, Concert Favorites #2, Ragtime Classics, Old Fashion Sing-Along, Occasions & Functions, Broadway Favorites, Christmas Favorites. MIDI-MI-NUS-ONE: Complete music packages including manual: Traditional Jazz, Dixieland Jazz, Jazz Standards, Jazz Waltz, Latin Jazz, Standard, Straight & Hard Bebop. CALL MAC-MIDI SOFTWARE: 1-617-598-8929 for details and pricing.

CONCERTWARE VERSION 4.

ConcertWare+ is a music program with three integrated parts: Music Writer, the Instrument Maker, and the Music Player. Great Wave Software; 5353 Scotts Valley Drive, Scotts Valley, CA 95066, 408-438-1990. Call for pricing.

MUSICWRITER.

Using the MusicWriter you can enter sheet music or original music by using the Mouse or the Macintosh Keyboard. Scores can be printed with full support for the ImageWriter, LaserWriter, and the Adobe Sonata fonts. Great Wave Software, 5353 Scotts Valley Drive, Scotts Valley, CA 95066, 408-438-1990. Call for pricing.

INSTRUMENTMAKER.

The InstrumentMaker lets you design your own instrumental sounds or modify any which come on the disk. Great Wave Software, 5353 Scotts Valley Drive, Scotts Valley, CA 95066, 408-438-1990. Call for pricing.

MUSICPLAYER.

The MusicPlayer combines music from the MusicWriter with instruments from the InstrumentMaker and plays back your full length selections through the Macintosh. It can also be played through a home stereo system for optimal sound. Great Wave Software, 5353 Scotts Valley Drive, Scotts Valley, CA 95066, 408-438-1990.

CONCERTWARE+ MIDI VERSION 4.

ConcertWare+MIDI includes all the features of ConcertWare and many more. MIDI stands for Musical Instrument Digital Interface. Using a MIDI adapter and ConcertWare+MIDI your Macintosh can control a MIDI compatible electronic keyboard, synthesizer or drum machine. Great Wave Software, 5353 Scotts Valley Drive, Scotts Valley, CA 95066, 408-438-1990. Call for pricing.

TERPSICHORE.
Great Wave Software now provides an extraordinary addition to the ConcertWare and family of music software called Terpsichore that is a collection of Renaissance/Baroque music. The 181 music files on these disks are designed exclusively for use with ConcertWare and ConcertWare & MIDI, and enable much of this music to be heard for the first time. Over 80% of these pieces have never before been recorded in any form. Great Wave Software, 5353 Scotts Valley Drive, Scotts Valley, CA 95066, 408-438-1990. $49.95.

PROFESSIONAL COMPOSER.
Professional Composer offers musicians and copyists creative power which surpasses that of far costlier systems. Sophisticated musical composition. Comprehensive editing. Performance-quality output. And musically intuitive operation. Mark of the Unicorn, 222 Third Street, Cambridge, MA 02142, 617-576-2760. $375.

PERFORMER V 2.0.
A recording studio at your fingertips. Performer is a powerful MIDI sequencer, editor, and performance tool for the Apple Macintosh 512K computer. Mark of the Unicorn, Inc., 222 Third Street, Cambridge, MA 02142, 617-576-2760. $310.

MUSIC MOUSE.
By using computer logic to assist with harmony, Music Mouse lets the player's musical sensitivity and imagination express themselves. This popular program can be used for the beginner to advanced musicians; for Macintosh128K and upwards and the sound outputs through the computer's built-in speaker or through any Macintosh MIDI interface, to external synthesizers and speakers. Opcode Systems, 444 Ramona, Palo Alto, CA 94301, 415-321-8977. $60.

OVALTUNE.
OvalTune is a new kind of program which generates music and images in response to mouse gestures. Improvisational painting. Opcode Systems, 444 Ramona, Palo Alto, CA 94301, 415-321-8977. For Macintosh Plus and SE and Macintosh II $199 Strawberry OvalTune $199.

DELUXE MUSIC CONSTRUCTION SET (VERSION 2).
The ultimate music tool for composing, performing, and publishing. Complete music notation tools, MIDI features, complete music playback and editing tools, and desktop music publishing. Opcode Systems, 444 Ramona, Palo Alto, CA 94301, 415-321-8977. $100.

OPCODE SEQUNECER 2.5.
Opcode's sequencer is a powerful real-time performance and composition system for the Apple Macintosh computer. Through the use of MIDI, the Macintosh turns into a cost effective 32 track recording studio with numerous special features not found in tape recorders or other computer based recording systems. Opcode Systems, 444 Ramona, Palo Alto, CA 94301, 415-321-8977. $250.

DIFFERENT DRUMMER.
Different Drummer uses digitally recorded sampled sounds for realistic recreations of instruments. No additional hardware, other

than a Mac 512K, Plus, or SE, is required. Just tap your beat on the Mac number pad or click and drag notes into place. An external drive and speaker is recommended. Primera Software, 650 Cragmont; Berkeley, CA 94708, 415-525-3000. $99.95.

DRUM FILE.
MIDI Librarian translator. Blank Software, 1034 Natoma St., San Francisco, CA 94103, 415-863-9224. $295.

JAM FACTORY.
Music improvisation and live-performance processor. Intelligent Music, PO Box 8748, Albany, NY 12208, 518-434-4110. $150.

LISTEN 2.0.
Musical-ear training with MIDI. Imaja, P O Box 638, Middletown, CT 06457, 203-347-5909. $69.

M.
Music composition. Intelligent Music, PO Box 8748, Albany, NY 12208, 518-434-4110. $200.

MUSICTYPE 2.0.
Music notation. Shaherazam, PO Box 26731, Milwaukee, WI. 53226, 414-442-7503. $59.95.

MUSICWORKS.
Music composition. Hayden Software, a division of Spinnaker Software Corp., 1 Kendall Sq., Cambridge, MA 02139, 617-494-1222. $49.95.

SOFTSYNTH 2.0.
Digital additive/FM synthesis software MS004. Digidesign, Inc., 1360 Willow Rd., Suite 101, Menlo Park, CA 94025, 415-327-8811. $295.

Q-SHEET.
SMPTE/MIDI Time Code-based MIDI automation software. Digidesign, Inc., 1360 Willow Rd., Ste. 101, Menlo Park, CA 94025, 415-327-8811. $495.

JAM SESSION.
Unique jamming instrument program by Broderbund. Call ComputerWare for ordering and information. 415-323-7559.

STUDIO SESSION.
Through digital recorded sounds, you can turn your Mac into a music machine. Play or create your own music by entering notes and selecting pre-defined instruments. Created by Bogas Productions. Call MacWARE-HOUSE for pricing and ordering: 800-255-6227.

MACRECORDER.
Hardware/software package that will allow you to record external sounds into digital data files in mono or stereo. Created by Farallon. Call ComputerWare for ordering and information 415-323-7559 or MacWAREHOUSE 800-255-6227.

MUSIC PUBLISHER.
Music printing software by Graphic Notes. Call ComputerWare for ordering/information, 415-323-7559.

PRACTICA MUSICA.
Unique music software that teaches how to identify two types of musical sounds: intervals and chords as well as elements of music theory related to intervals and chords. The software will play through the Mac or a MIDI keyboard by ARS Nova Software.

Call ComputerWare for ordering/information 415-323-7559 or MacWAREHOUSE 800-255-6227.

ROLAND D50 EDITOR/LIBRARIAN.
MIDI editor/librarian software for use with the Roland D50 series synthesizer by Zero One Research. Call ComputerWare for ordering/information, 415-323-7559.

APPLE II, AND GS HARDWARE.

PASSPORT MIDI INTERFACE.
The industry standard MIDI interface with MIDI IN, OUT, and DRUM OUT. Passport Designs, 625 Miramontes St., Half Moon Bay, CA 94109, 415-726-0280. Apple II plus, IIe, GS, $130.

PASSPORT MIDI INTERFACE.
The industry standard MIDI interface with MIDI IN,/OUT, and DRUM OUT and TAPE SYNC. Passport Designs, 625 Miramontes St., Half Moon Bay, CA 94109; 415-726-0280. Apple II plus, IIe, GS, $200.

PASSPORT MIDI PRO INTERFACE.
MIDI interface for the Apple IIc and Laser computer. No modification; includes full sync capabilities MIDI IN/OUT, Clock IN/OUT and Tape Sync IN/OUT. Passport Designs, 625 Miramontes St., Half Moon Bay, CA 94109, 415-726-0280. $200.

AUDIO ANIMATOR MUSIC BOARD.
A MIDI interface with a MIDI THRU port for sampling and editing MIDI data. Applied Engineering, PO Box 5100, Carrollton, TX 75011. Call 214-241-6060 for complete product information.

THE PHASOR.
An add-on sound card equipped with 12 simultaneous sound channels, 4 white noise generator, and a voice channel expandable to two voices. Comes with its own software, Applied Engineering, P.O. Box 798, Carrollton, TX 75006. Orders, call 214-241-6060. Call information and technical support for details 214-241-6069. $149.

APPLIED SONIC BLASTER.
CDA Computer Sales, One CDA Plaze Rt. 513, P.O. Box 533, Califon, NJ 0783. Call 800-526-5313, NJ 201-832-9004.

APPLIED AUDIO ANIMATOR.
CDA Computer Sales, One CDA Plaze Rt 513, P.O. Box 533, Califon, NJ 0783. Call 800-526-5313, NJ 201-832-9004.

CONSERVER.
The Conserver is an intergrated unit that provides six AC outlets, surge protection and a cooling fan. The unit acts as both a monitor stand and as a holder for one or two Apple 3.5-inch disk drives. Circulating air provides cooling for the GS when two or more add-on cards are placed in the expansion slots of the GS. Control buttons in front snaps all devices on and off conveniently. MDIdeas, Inc., 1163 Triton Dr., Foster City, CA 94404, 415-573-0580. $149.95.

SYSTEM SAVER IIGS.
Surge suppression, cooling fan, device. The Kensington System Saver IIGS protects your valuable GS and circuitry from dangerous power surges and spikes. Control buttons in front snaps all devices on and off conveniently with four A/C outlets that allow for monitor, printer, hard drive, etc., to

be regulated. Sold through Apple dealers, or call: 800-535-4242, NY 212-475-5200 for info. $99.95.

JUICE BOX GS SURGE SUPPRESSOR/ FAN.
Provides the IIGS with voltage protection, quiet fan for cooling, and three power outlets for peripherals with automatic switching. Attaches on the side of the GS. Orange Micro, Inc., 1400 N. Lakeview Ave., Anaheim, CA 92807. Call 800-223-8029, CA 714-779-2772.

SUPERSONIC STEREO CARD.
A digitized stereo output card that uses the DOC of the Apple IIGS to output true stereo. Any sound in GS software that addresses the DOC will have output in stereo. External speakers are recommended. Installs easily and can be snapped in most any slot to drive two 8-ohm mini speakers or headphones. MDIdeas, Inc., 1163 Triton Dr., Foster City, CA 94404, 415-573-0580. $59.95.

DIGITIZER.
The Supersonic Digitizer is a two-channel audio digitizer that inputs audio into the Ensoniq sound chip (DOC) via CD player or any other audio source. The Digitizer can record, edit, save and playback voices, music and sound waveforms. It plugs directly into the SuperSonic stereo card expansion connector (piggyback). MDIdeas, Inc., 1163 Triton Dr., Foster City, CA 94404, 415-573-0580. $59.95.

DIGITIZER PROFESSIONAL.
A stand-alone output/digital recorder add-on card, compatible with the Ensoniq sound chip (DOC) and the SuperSonic stereo card. Software controlled functions allow for pan-ning and fading effects during digitizing also includes special DNR (Digital Noise Reduction circuitry). MDIdeas, Inc., 1163 Triton Dr., Foster City, CA 94404, 415-573-0580. Digitizer Professional $149.95 *(Digitizer trade up is available)*.

FUTURESOUND STEREO DIGITIZER CARD.
A stand-alone stereo output/digital recorder add-on card. This hardware/software package will allow the user to control the sounds of the internal sound chip of the GS and also serves as a stereo card. This device will record from any sound source in mono or stereo: microphone, CD, tape player, etc. The software will edit sound waves for seperate tracks, looping, splicing, and even special effects (microhone included). Applied Visions, Inc., 1 Kendall Sq., Ste. 2200, Cambridge, MA 02139, 617-494-5417. $279.

SOUNDACE.
Digitizer stereo board for the GS. Parallax, Inc., 5249 Locust Ave. Carmichael, CA 95608. 916-721-5451. $44.95.

OCTORAM.
An expandable memory card for the Apple IIGS. (256K to 8 MB). When you need more internal storage space, OctoRam expands to store graphic, sound, and text/files. MDIdeas, Inc., 1163 Triton Drive; Foster City, CA 94404, 415-573-0580.

APPLE IIGS MEMORY EXPANSION CARD.
Memory board expandable to one MB using additional memory in 256K allotments. Apple Computer, Inc., 20525 Mariani Ave., Cupertino, CA 95014, 408-996-1010. $129.

APPLE HARD DISK 20SC.
Apple hard drive that provides 20 MB of data storage; works with the AppleII SCSI Card and Cable. Apple Computer, Inc. 20525 Mariani Ave, Cupertino, CA 95014, 408-996-1010. Apple IIGS, Apple SCSI Card, System Cable, $1,019.

CMS SERIES HARD DISK SYSTEM.
SCSI hard drives. Apple IIGS and Apple II ProDOS 8/ProDOS 16. SC20/Compact Series, CMS Enhancements Inc., 1372 Valencia Ave., Tustin, CA 92680, 714-259-9555.

CHINOOK HARD DRIVES.
Hard drives for all Apple II computers; prices vary. Call for details: Chinook Technology, Inc., 601 Main Street #635, Longmont, CO 80501, 303-678-5544, 800-727-5544.

FIRST CLASS PERIPHERALS HARD DRIVES.
Hard drives for Apple II computers: 20, 40, 60, 90 MB. Prices range from $595 to $2495. Call 800-982-3232 for complete product information.

HYPERDRIVE FX/20.
An external SCSI hard disk drive for the Apple IIGS with 20 MB for data storage. The FX/20 uses the Apple II Conversion kit and the SCSI add-on card. General Computer Corp., 215 First St., Cambridge, MA 02141, 800-634-9737. $1,199.

PLUS HARD DISK SYSTEMS.
Hard disk storage of 20, 30, 45, or 60 MB for an Apple IIGS through the SCSI port. A backup system is also recommended and available. MacPeak Systems, 1201 Spyglass, Austin, TX 78746, 512-327-3211. $1,095 and up

WESTERN DIGITAL HARD DRIVES.
Platinum-colored hard drives in 20-megabyte and 40 megabyte. Western Digital Corporation, 2445 McCabe Way, Irvine, CA 92714, 714-863-0102. Prices vary from $895 to $1195.

GS-RAM & GS-RAM PLUS.
Apple GS extended memory boards. Organize your GS! Call for pricing: 2 MB expander. Applied Engineering, PO Box 5100, Carrollton, TX 75011, 214-241-6060.

GSX.
Add-on board that increases the internal operating speed of the Apple GS to run 5.6 times faster. An important upgrade. Call for price and availability. MDIdeas, Inc., 1163 Triton Dr., Foster City, CA 94404, 415-573-0580.

MULTIRAM GS.
Memory board for expansion of the Apple IIGS, adding from 256K to 2 MB. Checkmate Technology Inc., 509 S. Rockford Dr., Tempe, AZ 85281, 800-325-7347 or 602-966-5802. Call for details and pricing information. .

MACINTOSH MIDI HARDWARE and MISCELLANEOUS.

MIDI TRANSPORT.
The MIDI Transport is Passport's dual MIDI interface for the Macintosh family of computers. It incorporates SMPTE to MIDI Time Code conversion, Direct Time Lock, and other professional features. The MIDI Transport will run with existing software

packages including Master Tracks Pro and Cue Sheet that incorporate MIDI Time Code plus Direct Time Lock for use with Performer. Passport, 625 Miramontes St., Half Moon Bay, CA 94019, 415-726-0280.

MINI-8.
The new serial port standard for Apple computers. The Mini-8 MIDI interface interconnects your Apple computer and up to 3 electronic musical synthesizers. Glimpse Waters Applications Company, 400 East 77th St., Suite 14J, New York City, NY 10021, 212-744-0080.

STUDIO PLUS TWO INTERFACE.
The Studio Plus Two gives your Macintosh two MIDI IN's and six MIDI OUT's. Opcode Sytems, 444 Ramona, Palo Alto, CA 94301, 415-321-8977. $275.

PROFESSIONAL PLUS INTERFACE.
The Professional Plus Interface attaches to the Modem Port or Printer Port on the Macintosh. It provides one MIDI IN and three MIDI OUTs which may be connected to any synthesizer, drum machine or other MIDI device using standard MIDI cables. Opcode includes cables for either the Macintosh 512K, Macintosh Plus, SE. Opcode Sytems, 444 Ramona, Palo Alto, CA 94301, 415-321-8977.

PASSPORT MIDI INTERFACE FOR THE MACINTOSH.
Provides MIDI IN and MIDI OUT to the Macintosh. (Available for Macintosh 512e, Macintosh Plus, Macintosh SE and Macintosh II) Passport Designs: 625 Miramontes Street, Half Moon Bay, CA 94109, 415-726-0280. $129.95.

DIGIDESIGN SOUND ACCELERATOR FOR THE MAC SE OR II.

This professional add-on card turns your Mac SE or II into a high-fidelity digital digitizer for true sampling. Digidesign, 1360 Willow Road, Suite 101, Menlo Park, CA 94023. Call 800-333-2137 or 415-327-8811 for details.

IMPULSE AUDIO DIGITIZER WITH SOUNDWAVE.
This combination of hardware and software will add a new features to your Macintosh— a digital audio recorder with full editing features. Take sound samples from external sources and create your own effects. Impulse Software. Call ComputerWare 415-323-7559 for ordering and information or MacWAREHOUSE 800-255-6227.

MACINTOSH PLUS MIDI ADAPTER CABLE.
Required to use the Passport MIDI Interface for Macintosh on a Macintosh Plus, Macintosh SE, or Macintosh II. Passport Designs, 625 Miramontes Street, Half Moon Bay, CA 94109, 415-726-0280. $25.

APPLE MIDI INTERFACE.
Includes one MIDI in-plug and one MIDI out-plug. Apple Computer, Inc., 20525 Mariani Ave., Cupertino, CA 95014, 408-996-1010. Also available through local Apple dealers. $99.

MIDI CABLES.
Used to connect your MIDI instruments to each other and to the Passport MIDI Interface. Passport Designs, 625 Miramontes Street; Half Moon Bay, CA 94109, 415-726-0280 or any MIDI equipment dealer. $25.

MIDIBOOST.
A significant boost for MIDI to run cables

more than 50 feet. Allows MIDI signals to be transmitted using XLR-type connectors and standard audio cables. $199 per pair. Marquis Music, 8439 Sunset Boulevard. Suite 408, Los Angeles CA 90069, 416-595-5498 for details.

DUST COVERS FOR APPLE COMPUTERS.
Protects Apple computers, monitors.

Kensington Microwave Ltd. 251 Park Ave., New York, NY 10010. 800-535-4242 or 212-475-5200. $13.75.

Co-Du-Co., 4802 W. Wisconsin Ave., Milwaukee, WI 53208, 414-476-1584. $24.95.

Computer Cover Company, 23352 Peralta, Suite 14, Laguna Hills, CA 92653, 800-235-5330, CA 800-237-5376.

MINI AMPLIFIED SPEAKER SYSTEMS.
Plug in wall amplified speakers for Apple II's and Macintosh.

BOSE ROOMMATE POWERED SPEAKER SYSTEM GS.
The Bose RoomMate speaker systems have been made exclusively for the Apple IIGS. The true digital sound of the GS can be heard with high quality and volume. Plug into the earphone jack on the GS or the add-on stereo sound card connectors for reasonable quality sound. See your local Apple dealer. $229.

SOUND SYSTEM 2.
Thunderous amplified speaker set. Built in

advanced design amplifier, volume control, 2-way super heterodyne speaker, noise filtering, Apple compatible, includes complete documentation. Use for Apple IIGS, IIe, IIc, II+, and Macintosh. NEXO Distribution, 914 East 8th Street, Suite 109, National City, CA 92050. 619-474-3328. $129 *(Tight budget alternative)*

YAMAHA DM-01 DUAL-POWERED SPEAKER SET.
Apple IIGS speaker system with two, four-inch drivers and a 5.5 watt amplifier. Each speaker is equipped individually with volume and low-boost tone controls. Yamaha Music Corporation, USA, 6600 Orangethorpe Buena Park, Ca 90620-1396. Call 714-522-9240. $99.95. *(Tight budget alternative)*

MIDI STARTER SYSTEM FOR THE IBM PC, XT, AT.
MIDI interface, sequencer, editor/librarians, and utility software. Check for compatibilty with your specific MIDI device. Music Quest, Inc. 1700 Alma Drive, Suite 260, Plano, TX 75075, 214-881-7408.

CHAPTER SIX
RESOURCES
FOR PURCHASING & DEVELOPMENT

Computer, MIDI Catalogs And Dealer Resources
MIDI Equipment And Instrument Manufacturers
MIDI Instrument Dealers
MIDI Books And Technical Books
MIDI Videos, Consulting, And Periodicals
MIDI Associations
MIDI And Telecommunications

RESOURCES FOR PURCHASING
AND DEVELOPMENT

This section is a comprehensive listing of the leading suppliers, dealers, manufacturers, media, professional resources, and other support information for your continued development. *Telephone numbers maybe subject to change without notice.*

COMPUTER, MIDI CATALOGS AND DEALER RESOURCES:
SOUND MANAGEMENT: Is a MIDI book publisher and an authorized dealer for Passport, Opcode, Sonus, Pyware, and many other MIDI manufacturers of Apple II, GS, Mac, Commodore, IBM, and Atari ST MIDI software, hardware, & keyboards. Call for catalog and discount orders at 800-548-4907. Sound Management, P. O. Box 3053, Peabody, MA 01961.

APPLE IIGS: THE BUYER'S GUIDE
Quarterly magazine with hundreds of Apple IIGS products and reports, 660 Beachland Blvd., Vero Beach FL 32963, 407-231-6904.

CDA COMPUTER SALES.
Complete Apple II, GS product distributor and music/sound products. Call for free catalog CDA Computer Sales, One CDA Plaza, Route 513, Califon, NJ 07830, 800-526-5313, NJ 201-832-9004.

THE CODA CATALOG.
Wenger Corporation, Music Learning Division, 1401 E. 79th Street, Bloomington, MN 55420-1590. Telephone: 800-843-1337. The $7 catalog is a large collection of music software.

COMPUTER MUSICIANS COOPERATIVE.
International cooperative, buying resource; membership $75, 3010 N. Sterling Avenue, Peoria, IL 61604. Call 309-685-4843 for complete details.

COMPUTERWARE.
The MacSource for Macintosh software and hardware; (Great selection of Mac + music sotware). Store: 490 California Avenue, Palo Alto, CA 94306, 415-323-7559. Small Business Sales, 800-323-1133 CA, 800-235-1155. International Sales 415-496-1003. Call for product listings.

DIGITAL ARTS & TECHNOLOGIES.
Complete music and MIDI software catalog. Department EMD, P.O. Box 11, Milford, CT 06460, 203-874-9080.

DR. T'S PRODUCT CATALOG.
Up-to-date music software, 220 Boyston Street, Suite 306, Chestnut Hill, MA 02167, 617-244-6954.

FUTURE MUSIC CATALOG.
A great purchasing and information resource for MIDI equipment, and other related items, 1-800-FOR-MIDI, or 1-702-359-6434. Address: P.O. 1090, 1465 Terminal Way, Reno, NV 89504.

GOLDEN GATE COMPUTING.
Apple IIc, plus, e, GS hardware and software dealer. Up-to-date GS music and sound hardware/systems. 722 Lombard Street, Suite 201, San Francisco, CA 94133, 800-548-9712.

GRAPHIC NOTES INC.
Macintosh music publishing, 200 Seventh Ave, Santa Cruz, CA 95062. Telephone: 408-476-0147.

MACCONNECTION.
A leading Macintosh hardware and software distributor for all Macintosh products; overnight delivery. Call 800-MAC & LISA, 800-622-5472, 603-446-7711.

MACWAREHOUSE.
A leading Macintosh hardware and software distributor for all Macintosh products. Call 800-255-6227 for catalog and/or ordering.

MIX BOOK SHELF CATALOG.
The recording industry resource center; a leader in support information, music software, editor, patch, and sound libraries, plus a variety of music references; including books, videos, and equipment manuals, call 800-233-9604 or 415-653-3307. Address: 2608 Ninth Street, Berkeley, CA 94710.

MICRO MUSIC CATALOG.
Micro MusicSM, Pinetree Plaza, 5269-20 Buford Highway, Atlanta, GA 30340. Telephone: 404-454-9646—competitive, up-to-date MIDI computer software, interfaces, and accessories.

MUSIC SOLUTION.
One of the most complete selections of music software for MIDI, 14760 Ventura Boulevard, Sherman Oaks, CA 91403. Call 800-442-MIDI, CA or 818-501-6929.

MUSICATION CATALOG.
1600 Broadway (48th Street), NY, NY 10019, Suite 1000A, 212-957-9100. MIDI software, interfaces, music printing, education software, MIDI instruments, and equipment.

MIDI MOUSE MUSIC.
Box 877-EB, Welches, OR 97067. Digital sound samplings and voice librarians, etc. Telephone: 503-622-4034.

PASSPROT DESIGNS SOFTWARE AND ACCESSORIES CATALOG.
A leader in MIDI software and interface devices: Passport Designs, 625 Miramontes Street, Half Moon Bay, CA 94109, 415-726-0280.

PROGRAMS PLUS.
A leading distributor of Apple II and Macintosh products. Call 800-832-3201.

THE SONUS PRODUCT CATALOG.
Leading software options and product information, 818-702-0992.

ZIMCO INTERNATIONAL, INC.
Leading product distributor for most types of computer hardware, drives, printers, software, parts, accessories, etc. ZIMCO, 85-39 213 Street, Queens Village, NY 11427.

800-227-6647 orders, 718-479-7888 and inquires.

MIDI EQUIPMENT AND INSTRUMENT MANUFACTURERS.

ALESIS CORPORATION.
A manufacturer of MIDI drum machines. Alesis Studio Electronics, 3630 Holdrege Avenue, Los Angeles, CA 90016. Call 213-467-8000 for product information.

BROSS PRODUCTS.
A manufacturer of MIDI guitar products. Bross Products, 7200 Dominion Circle, Los Angeles, CA 90040. Call 213-685-5141 for product details.

CASIO, INC.
A manufacturer of MIDI and non-MIDI keyboards, synthesizers, and other MIDI devices. Professional Music Products Division, 15 Gardner Road, Fairfield, NJ 07006 and Casio, Inc. 570 Mt. Pleasant Avenue, Dover NJ 07801. Call 201-361-5400 for product information and nearest dealer.

ENSONIQ CORPORATION.
A manufacturer of MIDI keyboards and samplers, 155 Great Valley Parkway, Malvern, PA 19355. Call 215-647-3930 for product information.

FOSTEX.
Leading manufactuers of multi-track recorders for the music industries. Call for details and ask about the E-Series of professional tape recorders, 15431 Blackburn Avenue, Norwalk, CA 90650, 213-921-1112.

KAWAI AMERICA CORPORATION.
A manufacturer of all MIDI devices. Department EM, 2055 East University Drive, Compton, CA 90224-9045. Call 213-631-1771 for product information.

KORG USA.
A manufactuer of many MIDI instruments and other MIDI products, 89 Frost Street, Westbury, NJ 11590. Call 800-645-3188 for product information.

OBERHEIM.
A manufacturer of many MIDI instruments and MIDI products, 2015 Davie Avenue, Commerce, CA 900401, 213-725-7870.

OPCODE SYSTEMS.
A manufacturer of MIDI interfaces and other MIDI products, 1024 Hamilton Court, Menlo Park, CA 94025, 415-321-8977 for product information.

PASSPORT DESIGNS, INC.
A manufacturer of MIDI interfaces for most computers, 625 Miramontes Street, Suite 103, Half Moon Bay, CA 94019. Call 415-726-0280 for product information.

ROLAND CORPORATION/US.
A manufacturer of MIDI instruments and other MIDI products, 7200 Dominion Circle, Los Angeles, CA 90040. Call 213-685-5141 for complete product information.

SONUS.
A producer of MIDI sequencer software for most computers, 21430 Strathern Street, Suite H, Canoga Park, CA 91304. Call 818-702-0992 for product information.

TECHNICS.
A producer of electronic digital/MIDI keyboards. Call 800-424-7669 for the nearest dealer.

YAMAHA INTERNATIONAL CORPORATION A manufacturer of electronic products, MIDI instruments, and music lab equipment, Digital Music Instrument Division, PO Box 6600, Buena Park, CA 90622. Call 714-522-9011 for product information.

MIDI INSTRUMENT DEALERS.

COMPUTER MUSICIANS COOPERATIVE.
Membership required: $75/yr. Discount MIDI software/mail order. Very competitive pricing. Telephone: 309-685-4843, call for information.

CMS COMPUTER MUSIC SUPPLY.
MIDI supplies and accessories for IBM and compatibles. 382 N. Lemon, Walnut, CA 91789. Call 800-322-MIDI, CA 714-594-5051.

CTC'S MIDI MUSIC CONNECTION.
Dealer of MIDI equipment and music software, 211N. El Camino Real, Encinitas, CA 92024. Call 619-944-4444 for requests.

DADDY'S.
A large variety of name brand MIDI instruments, 165 Mass. Avenue, Boston, MA. 02115 Telephone: 617-247-0909.

FUTURER MUSIC.
Large variety of MIDI equipment and other related item. Call 1-800-FOR-MIDI, or 1-702-359, 367-826-6434. Address: P.O.

1090, 1465 Terminal Way, Reno, NV 89504.

LASALLE MUSIC.
Popular MIDI instruments and possible used MIDI instruments, 1116 Boylston Street, Boston, MA, 617-536-0066.

MANNY'S.
One of the largest professional resources for purchasing MIDI instruments, 156W 48th Street, Manhattan, NY, 212-819-0576.

MIDI BASS.
360 Systems, Dept. KE, 18740 Oxnard Street, Tarzanz, CA 91356.

RHYTHM CITY.
One of the largest electronic instrument MIDI dealer, 287 E. Paces Ferry Road, Atlanta, Georgia 30305. Call 404-237-9552 for any MIDI equipment needs.

SAM ASH MUSIC.
One of the largest professional resources for MIDI instruments, 160W 48th Street, Manhattan, NY, 212-719-2299.

STEVE'S QUALITY INSTRUMENTS.
Excellent variety of MIDI instruments and other MIDI gear, 18 Water Street, Danver, MA, 508-777-3221.

TEKCOM CORPORATION.
Mac-based MIDI systems for all user levels, 1020 N. Delaware Avenue, Philadelphia, PA 19125, 215-426-6700.

THOROUGHBRED MUSIC.
MIDI dealer of major brands of all equipment, 2204E Hillsborough Avenue, Tampa, FL 33610. Call 813-237-5597 for details.

WURLITZER. Complete line of MIDI in

struments as well as other musical gear, 360 Newbury Street, Boston, MA. Telephone: 617-437-1815.

MIDI BOOKS AND TECHNICAL BOOKS

These books, manuals, and reference guides offer comprehensive information about popular keyboards, synthesizers, and other MIDI devices. Equipment tech books are a very important reference for a specific line/series of synthesizers/samplers; tech books are usually an outstanding resource for immediate and continued development.

MIDI-IN's, OUT's & THRU's.
A reference guide for musicians, performers, educators, and computer enthusiasts, (available through MIX Bookshelf).

THE MIDI BOOK.
A resource for illustration and diagrams for setting up, (available through MIX Bookshelf).

MIDI FOR MUSICIANS.
A leading book/resource that discusses the electronc instrument evolution, how to make music with MIDI instruments, and other technical information. Call CODA or MIX Bookshelf to order.

THE MIDI HOME STUDIO.
By Howard Massey, an easy-to-read book for set up and use of a home MIDI system for recording. (MIX Bookshelf).

THE ELECTRONIC MUSICIANS DICTIONARY.
Craig Anderson, published by AMSCO. A very complete list of terms relating to the field of MIDI and music. Available through MIX Bookshelf Catalog.

THE CASIO CZ BOOK AND THE YAMAHA DX.
A series of user tech books available. See the CODA catalog or visit music equipment stores for availability.

BEGINNING SYNTHESIZERS/USING MIDI.
Two comprehensive guides and references toward better utilization of equipment. MIX Bookshelf Catalog.

ALEXANDER PUBLISHING BOOKS FEATURING MANY "HOW TO BOOKS." AND INSTRUMENT-SPECIFIC GUIDES.
MIX Bookshelf Catalog.

COMPOSERS AND THE COMPUTER.
A reference that discusses the trends in contemporary compositional thinking. MIX Bookshelf Catalog.

MUSICIANS GUIDE TO THE RECORDING STUDIO.
A user book to help understand the in's and out's of recording with MIDI equipment. Urbanix Corporation, 73R Middle Streeet, Woburn, MA 01801.

An up-to-date inventory of leading books and technical recording manuals are also available form Mix Bookshelf Catalog.

MIDI VIDEOS, CONSULTING, AND PERIODICALS

MIDI MADE EASY VIDEO.
(VHS, $60), offers a fifty-five minute demonstration and explanation of MIDI theory

and equipment. (Available through Musication).

Secrets of Analog and Digital Synthesis Video.
Visual demonstrations for performance and sound design on synthesizers. Mix Bookshelf Catalog.

STEVE POCARO'S VIDEO.
Tour a professional MIDI setup and watch how its done by the recording artists. Mix Bookshelf Catalog.(VHS, $44.95).

MACINTOSH, MIDI, & MUSIC VIDEO.
Limited availability. Macintosh Music Video, P.O. Box 8240, Beaverton, OR 97076. Call 800-538-9696, ext. 850.$9.95.

HANDS ACROSS THE BOARD VIDEO.
By Emmett Chapman, Stick Enterprises, 8320 Yucca Trail, Los Angeles, CA 90046. Call 213-656-6878 for details.

Specific VHS video tapes
Available for learning/lessons with leading musicians in the field: guitar, bass, keyboards, drums, MIDI, etc. MIX Bookshelf Catalog.

ARRANGING AND RECORDING FOR ELECTRONIC KEYBOARDS.
By Vinnie Martucci. Learn, create, improvise, program, arrange, record, and improve: six, one-hour instructional tapes plus book, $69. Send for catalog, complete listing of hundreds of instructional tapes. Call 800-33-TAPES. Send for information: Homespun Tapes, LTD., Box 694EM, Woodstock, NY 12498.

MIDI CONSULTANTS/LESSONS.

A variety of user-services/lessons/consulting sessions are available to customers who buy from reputable electronic music dealers. Most music stores (where you buy your MIDI equipment) offer courses or private lessons/tutoring for synthesizers and keyboards.

Private lessons and consulting range from $12 to $50 per half hour or full hour. MIDI lessons are commonly offered by music students enrolled at local music colleges; contact through music schools and music stores.

MIDI-TECH.
Toll-Free MIDI consulting and training. User and purchasing consulting for any MIDI work station. Call MIDI-TECH: 800-243-MIDI or 312-816-8154.

MIDWEST MIDI CONSULTANTS.
Expert MIDI consultants and product suggestions: Call 405-736-6676 for details.

SOUNDWARE CORP.
MIDI support and product suggestions, 200 Menlo Oaks Drive, Menlo Park, CA 94025. Call 415-328-5773 for details.

TEKCOM CORPORATION.
Mac-based MIDI systems for all levels of users, 1020 N. Delaware Avenue, Philadelphia, PA 19125. Call for product suggestions and support: 215-426-6700.

PERIODICALS FOR COMPUTERS, RECORDING, & MIDI.

ELECTRONIC MUSICIAN.
A leading publication for users and professionals that offers special coverage and reporting of new developments in the MIDI world, 6400 Hollis Street #12, Emeryville, CA 94608. Call 415-653-3307; or P.O. Box 3747, Escondido, CA 92025; available at newsstands.

HOME AND STUDIO RECORDING.
Resource periodical for recording. Music Maker Publications, 7361 Topanga Canyon Blvd., Canoga Park, CA 91393; available at newsstands.

INCIDER.
An Apple II user magazine, InCider, Subscription Dept., P.O. Box 58618, Boulder, CO 80322-8618. Call 800-525-0643, CO 303-447-9330; available at newsstands.

KEYBOARD MAGAZINE.
A popular publication for new styles of keyboards, equipment, and other related MIDI products. GPI Publications, 20085 Stevens Creek, Cupertino, CA 95014; available at newsstands.

MACUSER.
A leading magazine featuring Macintosh information and product line ups. MacUser, P.O. Box 56986, Boulder, CO 80321-6986. Call 303-447-9330.

MACWORLD.
The Macintosh magazine. Comprehensive magazine featuring all Macintosh products, MacWorld, P.O. Box 54529 Boulder, CO 80322-4529. Call 800-525-0643.

MIX.
Leading resource for electronic musicians. Mix Publications, 2608 Ninth Street, Berkeley, CA 94710.

MUSIC, COMPUTER, AND SOFTWARE
Great resource for electronic musicians. MCS Publications, 190 East Main Street, Huntington, NY 11743; available at newsstands.

MUSICIAN.
Excellent resouce for musicians. Amordian Press, Box 701, 31 Commercial Street, Gloucester, MA 01930.

MUSIC TECHOLOGY.
A MIDI user source. Music Maker Publications, 2608 Ninth Street, Berkeley, CA 94710.

PC MAGAZINE.
Leading magazine for IBM and compatible computers. Available at newsstands.

RECORDING ENGINEER AND PRODUCER.
A technical publication. Intertec Publishing, 9221 Quivera Road, P.O. Box 12901, Overland Park, KS 66202.

ROLAND USER GROUP MAGAZINE.
Resource for users of Roland products. Roland Corp. US, 7200 Dominion Circle, Los Angeles, CA 90040.

START.
Leading magazine for Atari ST and MIDI users. P.O. Box 1569, Martinez, CA 94553-9873. available at newsstands. Call 800-234-7001.

Other electronic music periodicals or quaterly publications are always available at newsstands or through dealers, manufacturers, and music stores.

MIDI ASSOCIATIONS.

ASSOCIATION FOR TECHNOLOGY IN MUSIC INSTRUCTION.
To help with instruction in MIDI and music applications, 121 Harrison Avenue South, Hopkins, MN 55343. Call 612-933-5290 for information.

COMPUTER MUSICIANS COOPERATIVE.
International cooperative, buying resource. Membership $75, 3010 N. Sterling Avenue, Peoria, IL 61604. Call 309-685-4843 for complete details.

THE INTERNATIONAL MIDI ASSOCIATION. (I.M.A.)
The I.M.A. is an international MIDI information network, offering a monthly newsletter, a MIDI hotline, and other important services and support. I.M.A. Individual membership is $40 per year: IMA, 11857 Hartsook St., N. Hollywood, CA 91607.

MIDI AND TELECOMMUNICATIONS: 300/1200/2400 BAUD WITH ELECTRONIC MUSIC/MIDI FORUMS.

Nationally there are many bulletin board services offering free-registration for MIDI user groups and services. Your modem, telecommunications software, and personal computer can open a whole new door for learning about MID and supply user support by power users of MIDI systems. Recently, a spread of computer virus within popular networks has become a major factor and concern. If you <u>download</u> a file you may be taking a chance.

****BBS telephone numbers change.*****

THE EAST COAST MIDI BULLETIN BOARD SYSTEM.
A resource created by and for music professionals. On-line technical/engineering MIDI support for Apple/MAC, IBM/Compatibles, Atari ST, and Commodore. Telephone: 516-928-4986/516-474-2450.

COMPUSPEC.
Electronic modem information system for learning and purchasing the leading MIDI/musical products. CompuSpec, Inc., 9765 Jefferson Plaza, Suite 3, Omaha, NE 68127. Call: 800-999-SPEC, (300/1200 BAUD). Voice: 402-592-0660.

CitiNet.
Boston, MA. New England's free on-line service available to anyone with a computer and a modem—an interactive information network. The Music Forum actually has Yamaha DX7 sound patches you can download. Boston CitiNet, 617-439-5699.

AMERICAN MIDI USER GROUP/ AMUG. Dallas, TX, Telephone: 214-250-2811.

ENIAC MIDI BBS. New York, (No 2400 baud rate) Telephone: 212-751-2347.

PROMIDI BBS.
Texas, (No 2400 baud rate), Telephone: 214-248-8530.

MUSICIANS DEN.
Colorado, Telephone: 303-321-6857.

CRAM-SOFT FIDO.
Florida, Telephone: 305-226-3310.

WALKSOFT I AND II.
Michigan, Telephones: 313-435/9905/7818.

NEBULA 2.
California, Telephone: 916-351-6193.

RIVER CITY OPUS.
California, Telephone: 916-362-6522.

DYNASOFT FIDO.
California, Telephone: 916-753-8788.
Virginia, Telephone: 703-620-6836.

FAMILY COMPUTER CENTER. Virginia, (No 2400 baud rate), Telephone: 703-644-8445.

Foreign Countries BBS MIDI Networks.

MIDICOM.
Quebec, Canada, (No 2400 baud rate), Telephone: 514-744-7354.

MIDILINE BBS.
Ontario, Canada, (No 2400 baud rate), Telephone: 613-966-6823.

MIDI MEDIA. Bordeaux, France, (No 2400 baud rate) Telephone: 11-33-56-79-06-09.

PAY MODEM BULLETIN BOARD SERVICES 300/1200/2400 BAUD WITH MIDI FORUMS.

BIX. One Phoenix Mill Lane, Peterborough, NH 03458. Telephone: 603-924-9281.

COMPUSERVE. Arlington Centre Blvd. P.O. Box 20212, Columbus, OH 43220. Telephone: 800-848-8199 or 614-457-8650.

DELPHI. 3 Blackstone Street, Cambridge, MA 02139. Telephone: 800-544-4005 or 617-491-3393.

GENIE. 401 North Washington Street, Rockville, MD 20850. Telephone: 800-638-9636 or 301-340-4000. (BBS usergroup for Apple IIGS.)

PC PURSUIT. C/O Telenet Communications Corp., 12490 Sunrise Valley Drive, Reston, VA 22096. Telephone: 703-689-6000 or 800-368-4215. Voice, 800-835-3001.

THE SOURCE. 1616 Anderson Road, McLean, VA 22102. Telephone: 800-336-3330 or 702-743-7500.

NEWLETTER.

Music, MIDI, and Your AppleII.
A new monthly newsletter to help you get the most out of your Apple II and music goals. One-year subscription $14.95. MMP Systems, 635 Lytton Ave., Palo Alto, CA 94301.

LIST OF COMPUTER AND ELECTRONIC MUSIC TERMS

LIST OF COMPUTER & ELECTRONIC MUSIC TERMS

The expanding presence of computers and musical electronics has increased the need for understanding basic terms within these fields. The following list of *Computer & Electronic Music Terms* is included to help electronic literacy.

ABSTRACT SYNTHESIS: The manipulation of waveforms in such a manner as to create new sounds not commonly heard in nature.

ADDRESS BUS: A communication line inside computer hardware along which the memory locations of data are sent.

AI: An acronym for artificial intelligence; the use of fifth generation programming applied thinking and reasoning for higher-level tasks, e.g., voice synthesis, auto-correction in music composition and sequencing.

AMPLITUDE: The magnitude of a voltage or waveform; volume.

ANALOG: Pertaining to data in which numerical information is represented by electrical signal in continuous form; opposite of digital data.

ASCII: An abbreviation for American Standard Code for Information Interchange. Text files can be stored as ASCII format so that other computer operating systems may be able to read them.

AUDIO PATCH BAY: A connector box used to patch all audio wires into one place.

AUTO-CORRECT/AUTOMATIC CHECK: A fuction of a sequencer or drum machine that will automatically correct/adjust the timing or rhythm of the composition; for rhythmic timing. Also know as "Quantizing."

BACKUP COPY: To make a second or an additional copy of data files for assurance.

BAUD/RATE: Used to determine the rate of speed at which communication data can be sent between devices.

BIT: A binary digit.

BUG: A hardware or software problem that causes processing failure.

BYTE: A group of eight bits. It takes one byte to store each letter of information.

CAI: An abbreviation for computer-assisted instruction; eductional software programming technique use for learning and training.

CHANNEL: In reference to one MIDI data path; the transmission of MIDI data/messages on any one of 16 routes. Each channel can be addressed to send and receive MIDI information.

CHIP: A very thin slice of silicon treated to store thousands of electrical circuits to form an integrated circuit.

CLOCK: The standard way to set a timing signal for the tempo of a music composition and playback recording. A sequencer (hardware or software) has a clock for the purpose of synchronizing tracks and MIDI data.

CONTROL BUS: A communication line along which control data flows.

CONTROLLER: A MIDI device with a dedicated function; controllers make no sound but convert and produce MIDI data sent to another MIDI devices that is mono or polyphonic; MIDI guitar controller, drum controller, keyboard controller, bass controller, wind instrument controller, MIDI motion sensor controller.

CMS: An abbreviation for computer music sytem; an organization of computer hardware, software, MIDI devices, and audio equipment used to generate digital sounds for music; also referred to as a computer-controlled music system or MIDI system.

DATA BUS: A communication line that transports program data.

DAISY CHAIN: A term used to described the serial connection of several MIDI devices to one another; the MIDI THRU port is used for this connection.

DELAY: A term which describes the interval of time required for the vibrato effect to be heard once the beginning of a note is played.

DIGITAL: Pertaining to data in the form of digits: 0's and 1's (on or off); opposite of analog.

DIGITIZE: To express/save/reuse data in a digital format.

DISK: Floppy or hard storage media; rotating material used to store bits of information.

DISPLAY: The visual picture seen on the monitor in color or black and white.

DOC: Digital Oscillator Chip; a 15 voice microelectonic chip found in every Apple IIGS.

DOUBLE-DENSITY/DOUBLE SIDED FLOPPY DISK: A disk that can store twice the amount of information and uses both sides for storage.

DRUM MACHINE: MIDI percussion (electronic percussion) device manufactured by the leading producers of MIDI equipment. A drum box is programmable and will produce quality drum sounds and rhythm patterns for use in a CMS.

DRUM SYNC and TAPE SYNC: The way to synchronize (start at the same time) MIDI drum data to a tape recorder.

EDIT: The process by which data is corrected: insert, delete, paste transpose, etc.

ELECTRONIC MUSICSHIP: The skill, ability, and artistry used to produce electronic generated music.

ELECTRONIC WIND INSTRUMENT: A MIDI wind instrument or controller that produces MIDI data..

ELEMENTS OF SOUND: Three distinct characteristics of every sound: pitch, timbre, and amplitude.

EQUALIZER: An audio device with levers and slide bars used to regulate and alter sound frequencies: the highs, lows, and midrange.

FEEDBACK: A high frequency noise when audio devices (microphone and speakers) are placed too close to one another.

FORMATTING: (Initializing) The process of preparing a disk to accept/receive information; includes laying down of data tracks on a disk.

GLITCH: A disturbance of electrical data that causes some variation of normal operation.

HARDWARE: A term used to describe a large variety of electronic components: the computer, add-on cards, printer, monitor, disk drives, MIDI equipment, audio equipment; all external peripherals.

HERTZ: A unit of frequency equal to one cycle per second.

HISS: An electrical generated disturbance/light noise causing audio and recording difficulties or background noise. Usually caused by a weak signal or faulty connections.

HUM: An electrical generated disturbance/deep noise causing audio and recording difficulties or background noise. Usually caused by weak or loose connection of wires, plugs, cables, adapters, or audio equipment.

INTERFACE: A method to share a boundry; to connect and then process.

IMITATIVE SYNTHESIS: To duplicate the sounds of traditional musical instruments and sounds.

JOYSTICK: An external input device that uses a movable lever with one or two buttons to press that activates the software.

LCD: A digital display screen consisting of a liquid crystal material between sheets of thin glass that become readable in the presence of an applied voltage. Usually found on a calculator, synthesizer, sequencer hardware, and drum machine.

LOW-PASS FILTER: To filter/remove unwanted high frequencies.

MENU: A pull-down or pull-up list of commands which appears on the monitor and allows for selection of specific operation.

MIDI: An acronym for Musical Instrument Digital Interface; a serial protocol that allows MIDI-equipped instruments and devices to communicate and to be compatible.

MIDI BOTTLE NECK: Also known as a MIDI recording choke; too much MIDI data being processed via sequencer or synth.

MIDI CABLES: A special 5- pin DIN cable used to connect MIDI devices. MIDI cables are available in a variety of lengths up to 50 feet.

MIDI CHANNEL: Similar to "CHANNEL," the path/route for MIDI data to travel; assignable MIDI channels are 1-16.

MIDI DELAY: Technical MIDI data transmission delay. Usually corrected by filtering device.

MIDI FILTER: MIDI device that can remove unwanted MIDI messages; e.g. aftertouch data.

MIDI IN: The standard port (5-DIN receptacle) used for connecting a MIDI devices to receive MIDI data; located on the rear panel of a MIDI-equipped instrument/device.

MIDI INTERFACE: The industry standard and a necessary component used to connect a computer to MIDI devices. A snap-in, add-on board, or a stand-alone device with MID IN/OUT. A MIDI interface allows a computer to send and receive MIDI information. All Apple II and Macintosh, Commodore, IBM, and compatible computers need a MIDI interface; Atari ST series have built-in MIDI interface ports ready for connection. (Standard MIDI interface hardware is available from: Apple, Passport, Opcode, Sonus).

MIDI MIXER: A MIDI device that combines two or more MIDI devices' output.

MIDI OUT: The standard port (5-DIN receptacle) used for connecting a MIDI devices to transmit MIDI data; located on the rear panel of a MIDI-equipped device.

MIDI SYNC DEVICE: A MIDI device that translates MIDI data to SMPTE data.

MIDI THRU: In addition to MIDI IN and MIDI OUT, a MIDI THRU port is a third MIDI receptacle/connector available only on some MIDI devices; it is used to connect MIDI equipment and devices in a series or daisy chain.

MIDI THRU BOX: MIDI connection hardware; junction box that allows a variety of MIDI devices to be connected; Yamaha MIDI Thru Boxes or JL Cooper Boxes-MSB16/20.

MIDI PATCHER: A device used for connecting and integrating; usually contains eight in and out MIDI routings and memory ability for patch sounds and switches.

MIDI SWITCH: An on or off switcher that can regulate MIDI data messages.

MODEM: An external hardware device or an internal add-on card used to connect a computer to a telephone line for communication with another computer and data bases.

MODULE: MIDI synthesizer or sampler with no keyboard; fits on a rack or shelf and generates, sends, and receives MIDI data; MIDI modules are used with synths and controllers and cost less money.

MODULAR PROGRAMMING: A method of sequencing MIDI data in sections; which then can be re-connected to the entire composition.

MONITOR: A television-type screen or CRT device used to receive computer output. The more pixels a monitor has the sharper the images appear.

MONOPHONIC: The way to describe a musical instrument that has only one sound.

MOUSE: A small hand-held external input device used for pointing and clicking to execute computer commands. A cursor/pointer/icon appears on the screen and by moving, pointing, and pressing a button on the mouse the software performs a task.

MULTITIMBRAL: The ability of some MIDI instruments to produce two or more different sounds or timbres. Multitimbral devices have 4 to 16 independent voices that can produce bass, string, percussion, and horn sounds simultaneously.

MULTI-TRACK: The technique used to record different musical parts separately which then are synchronized for playback.

MUSIC PRINTING: A print out of a composition in standard music notation; an important feature when selecting music composition software.

NOTATION SOFTWARE: Software that converts musicical data into sheet music.

OMNI MODE: A term used when a MIDI device is receiving on multiple MIDI channels, more than one MIDI channel.

OSCILLATOR: Pulse-generating microelectronic circuitry in which the frequency that the pulse is generated will determine the tone.

OUTBOARD DEVICES: Audio signal processors that will add reverb or other effects to audio signal for more dynamic acoustics.

QUANTIZATION: Auto-correct; a feature of some sequencers and drum machines that adjusts the rhythm to the nearest user-specified setting.

PARAMETERS: A series of control funtions used to set and select MIDI instrument sound data.

PANNING: The process of controlling and adjusting recorded instrument sounds; this feature is found in some digitizing software.

PARALLEL: Pertaining to the simultaneity of two or more processes.

PATCH: A specific sound or group of voices/sounds store in a MIDI instrument or on disk, cartridge, or in RAM/ROM.

PATCHING: The way to connect devices to one another.

PEAK: The loudest volume/amplitude.

PITCH: The relative position of a tone on a scale as determined by its frequency.

PIXEL: A tiny rectangular element used to form images on a monitor. The higher the number of pixels; the higher the quality of the screen's resolution.

POLY MODE: A term used when a MIDI device is receiving on one MIDI channel.

POLYPHONIC: The way to describe a multi-voice instrument. Capable of playing more that one note at one time.

PORT: The point of connection for in/out of devices.

PRE-SETS: A feature of MIDI and nonMIDI instruments which can be factory or user programmed; storage of previously sampled sounds or customized sound patches; for example, drum beats, wind instruments, steel drums or bass.

PROGRAM or SOFTWARE: A set of detailed instructions written in a computer language used to perform a specific task or application; commonly found on 5.25, 3.5, or CD ROM.

PUNCH IN OR OUT: The way to change a specific part of a composition; an important edit feature in sequencing or tape recording.

RAM: Read-write memory; available for use within the computer's memory board. Each software package requires different amounts of RAM.

REVERB EFFECT UNIT: A device used in a MIDI system that can add a variable echo effect to the musical data output; reverb effects can add character and natural deminisions to the electronic digital sound.

REAL TIME: A term used to describe actual time, live performance, or what is currently occuring. The easiest and most common method of recording a sequence of musical data.

ROM: Read-only memory used for permanent storage of data.

RUNNING STATUS: A feature of some MIDI devices/keyboards; a way of sending data bytes.

SAMPLED SOUND: A single sound or collection of preprogrammed or prerecorded real sounds. Digitizer hardware or a sampler keyboard can duplicate a sound source's parameters. To sample sound, such factors as sampling rate, volume, balance, frequency, and reverb are regulated. Sample sounds can be edited for instrument-based sound libraries--pianos, strings, leadlines, splits, brass, basses, speical effects, birds, nature sounds; formatted on data cassettes, RAM/ROM cartridges, 3.5 disks and computer specific floppy disks.

SCORE: The formal layout of musical notation for a piece of music.

SEQUENCE: A section or segment of music you enter into memory for editing and modification.

SEQUENCER/EDITOR: Computer software or dedicated hardware; a MIDI data recorder used to edit, compose, and playback musical data entered by step time or real time.

SERIAL INTERFACE: The type of connection over which one bit of data moves after the other on the same wire.

SIGNAL PROCESSOR: A device used in a MIDI system that can alter an audio signal; that is in reverb effects, delay, and compression. Multi-effects/signal processors can manipulate the audio signal in many ways.

SLAVE: In reference to the connection of two or more electronic instruments in which one, the master, controls/plays the other/s.

SLOT: Expandable internal computer hardware openings; the connection in which an add-on hardware card is snapped into. Slots can be identified by number or location on the motherboard.

SMPTE: The official timing standard and code used by the Society of Motion Picture and Television to sync audio to film/video productions.

SONG POSITION POINTER: A MIDI feature/command when synchronizing musical events to occur at the same time; setting the MIDI clock to coordinate the sequences and MIDI devices.

SOUND LIBRARIES: Very similar to voice librarians, in that a collection of patches, tones, or sounds (bank of 32) are prerecorded; sound libraries can be edited by changing the envelope. These libraries allow your computer or MIDI system to emulate a piano, violin, trumpet, and nature sounds.

SOUND PATCH EDITOR: Software sound editor used to alter presets and existing sound files for most leading synthesizers.

SOUND SAMPLING: To record external sounds directly into your computer or MIDI equipment for musical use, editing, and storage.

SOFTWARE: A term used for a computer program; music, word processing, and educational programs are available on 3.5, 5.25 size floppy disks.

SOFTWARE UPGRADES: Manufacturers of computer software announce new software upgrade versions to registered owners (free or for a small charge) with improvements and advanced features; e.g., V1.0 has been upgraded to V1.1, to V2.0 to V3.01, etc.

STEP TIME: The method used to enter musical data a section at a time.

SURGE SUPPRESSOR: A device for protection against A/C voltage spikes and interrupts. Some devices combine system cooling and voltage protection.

SYSTEM-EXCLUSIVE DATA: Two of the16 MIDI channels are reserved and dedicated to performance data that is distinct to specific equipment.

SYNC/SYNC TONE: An electronic tone used to coordinate MIDI devices by setting and controlling the clock.

SYNTHESIS: To produce artificially or to imitate; to duplicated the sounds of musical instruments; forms of synthesis include: additive, subtractive, phase distortion, FM and LA.

SYNTHESIZER: (Synth); MIDI equipment that can generate any sound by waveform. Synthesizers have keyboards or are keyboardless; sophistication, expense, sound quality, and ease of use are common considerations. Well-known manufacturers include: Korg, Roland, Yamaha, Fender, Casio, Ensoniq, E-MU Systems, Kurzweil, Fairlight CMI, Synclavier.

TAPE-SYNC: The technique used in tape recording; transferring of musical data from a computer to recorder.

TIMBRE: The quality of a sound that distinguishes it from other sounds of the same pitch and volume; the distinctive tone of a musical instrument, a voice.

TONE MIX: A feature or mode of some MIDI devices that enables two timbres to be played together.

TOUCH-SENSITIVE: The ability of some MIDI keyboards to respond to the user's touch of the keys; soft or heavier striking of the keys will result in soft or heavy sound responses.

TRACKS: In reference to the storage on the width of a tape; for sequencing software--the way musical data can be stored and routed to a variety of MIDI devices to produce different musical tasks.

TRANSCRIBER: Music software that will transfer real time data to the computer's memory for storage on disk, editing, or printing.

USER-FRIENDLY: A term used to describe an easy-to-use interface; e.g., easy-to-use software.

VOICE LIBRARIANS/VOICE PROGRAMS: Software with prerecorded instrument sound files that contain a variety of natural or abstract sounds used with specific MIDI instruments.

VIBRATO: The ability of an electronic device to add expression to a note by regularly varying the pitch.

WAVEFORM: The shape of the frequencies that produce a sound; e.g., triangle, sawtooth, square, pulse, sine, resonance wave.

WINDOW: A term used to describe the portion of a program's menu, seen on the monitor, used to execute a command.

WIND-TO-MIDI: MIDI controller that converts a wind instrument to MIDI data.

WRITE-PROTECTION: A system used to prevent erasure of data; every floppy disk has a write-protection lock system.

DATE DUE			
NO 14 '93			
GAYLORD			PRINTED IN U.S.A.